Memories of a Psychopath

Mary Metzger

Published by Mary Metzger, 2024.

MEMORIES OF A PSYCHOPATH

First edition. January 12, 2024.

Copyright © 2024 Mary Metzger.

ISBN: 979-8224741786

Written by Mary Metzger.

To Olga Kazatkina

The Memories of a Psychopath

Chapter 1: Ancient Memories

One of the most exciting developments in genetics is the discovery that we inherit our ancestors' memories and pass them on to future generations. Memories do not belong only to us but are part and parcel of the memory of the people to whom we belong.

I am a descendant of Jebe, who was one of Genghis Khan's Novans, or generals. The Secret History of the Mongols said, "They are the Four Dogs of Temujin. They have foreheads of brass, their jaws are like scissors, their tongues like piercing awls, their heads are iron, and their whipping tails swords. In the day of battle, they devour enemy flesh. Behold, they are now unleashed, and they slobber at the mouth with glee." These four dogs were Kublai (different from Kublai Khan), Jelme, Subotai, and Jebe.

The Mongols are renown for instituting a reign of psychological terror so deep in the hearts of their opponents that they would surrender rather than fight. Those who decided to fight were subject to no mercy. The destruction of Nishapur was a perfect example. Genghis Khan whose son-in-law was part of an envoy sent to negotiate with the people of Nishapur was put to death. This enraged the Khan, and the Mongols met the inhabitants of Nishapur with a brutality that had become a feature of Genghis Khan's conquests. He commanded that not a single inhabitant be spared. The streets of the thriving city ran red with blood as the army laid waste to everyone. In one single day, the Mongols slaughtered 1.7 million people. The Khan ordered that even cats and dogs should be obliterated. Then, Genghis Khan order the construction of a pyramid built with the heads of the murdered as a testament to his victory.

But the Mongols were not only savage barbarians; they also had a well-disciplined, well-trained organization of fighters who obeyed their ruler's commands unequivocally. Under the Emperor of All Men, the Master of Thrones and Crowns, and the Scourge of God—the

Mongols made war a business. The Khan took a loose federation of soldiers and turned it into an organized army based on iron discipline and meticulous attention to detail. He trained his men until they were mechanically perfect. Then, they set out to conquer the world in his name. So it was that every nation, every ruler, every potential enemy, meant that steps must be taken for its subjugation. Genghis Khan said, "As there is only one sun in Heaven, there should be only one Kha-Khan on Earth." There is no hint that Mongol domination should stop short of worldwide conquest.

The principles, doctrines, and personality of the Khan dominated his army. He allowed for no weakness, vulnerability, compassion, remorse, or regret for their actions. "Monasteries and temples breed mildness of character; remember, it is only the fierce and warlike who dominate." He hated ostentation and display. Years later, he would say: "For my own part, I detest luxury and practice moderation. I have only one coat and one food. I eat the same food as my humblest herdsman."

But when it came to women, he considered them a necessary part of the spoils of war. Geneticists have found that nearly eight percent of the men living in the former Mongolian empire region carry chromosomes identical to Genghis Khan. That translates to 0.5 percent of the world's male population, or roughly 16 million descendants living today. He not only conquered the world, but he also populated it.

With their cunning minds, the "Four Dogs of Temujin" lead the pack towards victory in the name of the Khan. They relied on specific, well-defined methods of battle that the Mongols used over and over again. Chief among these was the power of mobility, flexibility, and speed, for which the Mongols were famous. In addition, long, overnight marches bent on deceiving the enemy into believing that the main effort was coming from one direction when they were coming from another. Retreats that tuned into attacks when the enemy was busy focusing on other things.

One of their favorite tricks was that employed by Jebe in the battle for the Jin empire. Jebe retreats several hundred miles from the central battlefront, leaving a large amount of Mongol booty on the ground. The Chinese troops, unable to resist, paused to plunder it. Jebe's army returned, having ridden 100 miles in 24 hours to rout the undisciplined Jim forces and capture Liaoyan. It was not only the cleverness of their guise but the fact that they rode nearly 100 miles in 24 hours that made Jebe's successes.

So successful was Genghis in running his business and establishing his superiority that the warfare fundamentals of the Mongols were followed to the present. Though seemingly revolutionary, the German blitzkrieg of WW II was nothing new but had been used by the Mongols. Rommel and Patton used Khan's tactics. They are taught by the U.S. Army today. Genghis Khan and his armies accomplished feats that would be hard for modern armies to duplicate

About five years before he became the great Khan of the Mongols, Temujin, as he was known then, was fighting the Battle of the Twelve Sides or that battle of Chakirmaut as it is alternately known. Having united the eastern tribes of Mongolia, Genghis turned his attention to the west, which was blocked by the Naiman people and their allied tribes. Temujin had fewer warriors than those deployed by Tayan Khan, the leader of the Naimans, and his horses were weaker, having traveled long and hard. He tried to cover this up by building many campfires to make his soldiers appear more numerous. But Tayan Khan was not easily fooled and planned to withdraw his forces across the Altai Mountains. Tayan's reckless first son, Gulchulug, prevailed in the war council, and the army was sent on a frontal assault against the Mongols. Temujin's response was to keep them against the mountains at their rear. Then, Temujin sought to take advantage of their superior mobility by encircling the enemy and forcing them closer together to make them less effective than Jhe Mongols. He won the battle but was shot in the neck by a young soldier. Temujin, after he had recovered, asked the vanquish who shot his horse, not himself, in the neck. He said this either to hide his injury or possibly in an attempt to prevent false confessions. Jirqo'ada came forward and voluntarily confessed. He added that it was Temujin's right to kill him, but he could serve him loyally if allowed to live. Genghis valued loyalty above all else, and he pardoned him. He then gave Jirio'adai a new name, Jebe, which meant "arrow" in Mongolian.

The Borjigin and the Tayichiud tribes shared a common ancestor in Bodonchar Munkhag a renowned tribal chieftain and warlord. Khabul Khan of the Borjigin tribe designated Ambaghai of the Tayichiud as his successor. Thus, Ambaghai Khan became the second Khan of the Khamag Mongols. The rule of the Mongols had alternated between the Borjigid and Tayichiud tribes, finally coming into the hands of Genghis Khan of Borjigin. Both Genghis Khan and Jebe were directly related to Bodonchar Munkhag.

Jebe was part of the Besud clan of Tayichiud, but this did not stop Genghis Khan from welcoming him into the horde and, eventually, from making him one of his "four dogs." With his honesty, loyalty, and talents, Jebe climbed up the hierarchy of the Mongolian army. By age 25, Jebe was in command of the critical left wing of the military in the 1211 Jin invasion. He would prove himself over and over again as one of the greatest generals of all time.

In the Secret History of the Mongols, the Naimans who were Tayichiud, are portrayed as bitter enemies of Genghis Khan. In 1216, Genghis Khan dispatched Jebe to fight his enemy Kuchlug. When the Mongols approached, Kuchlug fled, unable to find support in Kashgar. He continued south, eventually reaching the border. A group of hunters caught him and handed him over to the Mongols, who beheaded him. Because of his victory, Jebe was crowned Naiman Beg or the Prince of the Naimans, a title passed on from father to son.

Genghis Khan was concerned with Jebe's success. He was still determining if Jebe would become more ambitious and rebel against him. When Jebe heard about this, he immediately returned to where Genghis Khan was and offered 100 white horses, the same kind that Genghis Khan rode when Jebe wounded him, as a sign of loyalty. After this, Jebe's commitment to Genghis Kahn was never to be doubted.

In 1219, Jebe and Subutai defeated the Georgians and conquered the Kievan Rus and Cumains at the Battle of the Kalka River. In 1224, Jebe died on his return. How he died is a subject of great debate, but Jebe left an indelible mark on history with his conquests in China, Central Asia, Europe, and Kyiv Rus.

Meanwhile, I was in Russia searching for the Boltuc side of the family. Through the internet, I made a lot of contacts with Boltuc family members who lived all over the world. One, a woman in Australia, had put together a family history, which dates back to the 16th Century. Through this, I connected with my cousin and his brothers who lived in Bialystok and, through him, with other family members. My cousin Jersey's grandfather, John Boltuc, was the brother of my grandmother. Mary. While my grandmother did not look Mongolian, except for her eyes, John was the image of a Mongol. I resemble him.

I visited the Belarussian Museum in London, where I learned much more about my grandmother's family and my grandfather's as well. On my grandfather's side, I belonged to one of the oldest Slavic families in Europe. We were Jasina's and had our own family crest under which we fought. But I found out little about the Boltucs except for the fact that they were, as the Priest said, "soldiers and police officers." This was, of course, a biased statement that belied his view of anything Mongolian. We were exactly, "soldiers and police officers." One of our ancestors was Milkolai Boltuc. During World War I, Boltuc served in the Tsarist Army. He fought with distinction in the Finnish War in 1918. After the Bolshevik Revoluton, he served as a captain in the White Russian Army during the Russian Civil War.

While fighting the Nazis in World War II, he was killed at the Battle of Lomianki by a sniper while he was leading the charge. According to written family records, he said while he was leaving home before the war, "This is not the war we are going to win, and I am not the kind of soldier who would surrender." I went to visit his tomb with my cousin Jerzy in Warsaw at the Pwazki Military Cemetery. I was very proud of being a warrior, of belong to the "soldiers and police officers" who bore the Boltuc name.

Mikolai Boltuc was prevented from rising to the rank of general was held back for several years, in part because of his anti-religious attitude. He was profoundly anti-religious as I am.

The majority of my family lived in and around Lida, Belarus. Boltuc was, moreover, not a Russian, Polish, or Lithuanian name but was rather Mongolian, as I had learned from my research. It means "to happen" in Mongolian. I was looking for the Boltuc name in Lida, Belarus when I stumbled upon Naiman Beg. I found that Naiman Beg was not his real name but a title that means "Prince of the Naimans." The person who wrote this suggested he was related to the Khan dynasty ruling Mongolia. It said that every "Naiman Beg" was a direct descendant of Jebe, who earned the title and passed it on from father to son.

Naiman Beg's ancestors came to the Grand Duchy of Lithuania at the beginning of the fifteenth Century as part of the Golden Horde. They came both to seek shelter against their enemies and to serve Vytautas the Great in his war against the Teutonic Knights. The Mongols took part in the Battle of Grunwald on July 15, 1410, and proved invaluable to the king. Afterward, most Mongols settled in the area of Lida and served as soldiers organized in troops, called up in need by Lithuanian rulers. They also received titles, are known collectively as Szlachta, and were considered part of the Polish Lithuanian nobility even though they were Monguls.

Then, I read the following: the body of warriors led by Naiman Beg was so large that it led to two banners: Naiman and Kongrat. Sons of Naiman Beg and later their male descendants were banner holders (commanders) of these units. The eldest son was possibly Piotr, as his descendants constantly took command over the Naiman Banner.

Naiman Beg had at least three sons: Piotr, Konwrat, and Olishko. Piotr and Konwrat are the progenitors of several Mongol families. However, Olishko is my direct ancestor, giving rise to the Bołciuks or Boltuc side of the family. Now, I could trace my family back to Naiman Beg.

My Grandmother was a Boltuc, born in Lida, Belarus. There are numerous Boltucs there, as Lida was given to the Mongols for their participation in the Battle of Grunwald. She came to America around 1880. I was her first living grandchild and lived with my grandparents for nearly seven years. My grandparents spoke very little English, and so, neither did I. I had no exposure to radio or TV for a long time, so my memories were untouched except for my family and the place I grew up in.

I do not know how far back my genetic memories go over time: I don't know how much Jebe I am. Even though I was a female, I had little interest in the toys that little girls play with. Instead, I always remember being a warrior even though I was too young to understand what a warrior was, and yet I knew myself as such. When I was married, I turned the basement into a gym surrounded by the great fighters of the time hanging above me; I skipped rope, did shadowboxing, and punched the speed bag. I thought as a warrior, I was always ready to fight.

From the time I was a child, I dreamed of having a horse. At first, my grandmother satisfied this by buying me a cardboard horse that hung over my shoulders, and I pretended to ride. This cardboard horse no longer sufficed, so my grandmother, at tremendous expenses for a woman of her means, bought me a horse made in the image of a live pony from FAO Schwartz. Horsehair covered the pony, and it had eyes made of blue marble. I called her Lacatoria and rode her day and night.

When it was too cold to go outside, I relied on my army of cowboys and Indians. My Grandfather had put a covering of clay on the bottom of a table, and I would sit and play with them for hours as my hordes overtook the hordes of others and killed them.

Much later, I understood that this was my outlook on life. In a war of "all against all," I sought to be a winner. There was no room for kindness but only for competition, as I struggled to make the world see I was superior. But the realization of all this took a long, long time. It took all of my life.

Chapter 2: Memories of a Psychopath

This is the autobiography of a psychopath, although it did not start that way. It started out as a simple autobiography. My friends and family had been asking me to write about my life: I had grown up in a poor coal mining town in Nanticoke, Pa., had begun life as a manual laborer, and went on to become a college professor. I have taught at New York University, Rutgers University, Kean University, and Hudson County Community College as a political scientist, a writing instructor, an English as a Second Language Instructor, and a teacher of rhetoric. I taught Physics and Philosophy at the Moscow Institute of Physics and Technology and Critical Thinking at the All-Russian Library for Foreign Literature. I had been married twice, once to a master carpenter and the second time to a hospital administrator. I had three children, five grandchildren, and two great-grandchildren. I studied cooking and started my own wholesale business, which made gourmet vegetarian foods for special diets. I had been politically active in left-wing causes and helped develop programs for daycare centers and battered women's shelters. I have traveled to over 35 countries. At 62, I went to Russia and spent sixteen years teaching there. When I was in Bishkek, Kyrgyzstan, on a cold winter day, covered with blankets, I sat at my computer and began to write my autobiography. In writing it, I discovered that I was a psychopath.

What I had written turned out to be not just a recollection of the history of my life but a journey of self-discovery in which I gradually came to understand my true self, the part I had kept hidden from the world and myself. I was surprised to find out that I was not a loving mother, a kind wife, a good employer, or a patient and gentle professor who helped others, but was, in fact, the very opposite of what I perceived myself to be: I found joy in inflicting physical and psychological pain on others with little or no compassion. I left behind my friends, family, lovers, and husbands and walk away from careers and jobs. I wander from place to place, always ready to go when insulted or humiliated. I did this to sustain my feelings of superiority and dominance.

While recalling and analyzing my life, I became acutely aware of the fact that I was an abnormal person in a world filled with more or less ordinary people; I was a psychopath who saw others only in terms of myself and my needs and not as human beings with needs and wants of their own. I realized that the words normal and abnormal are internally related, with the definition of one dependent on the existence of the other: one is normal, with empathy and compassion towards others, or abnormal, caring exclusively about one's own naked self-interest.

Because I am a Political Scientist, my attempts to define "normal" and "abnormal" human behaviors are conceived in the context of political theory. In classical political theory, this breaks down into a Hobbesian definition, emphasizing self-interest and self-preservation as the foundation of society, and the political theory of Rousseau or Marx, emphasizing compassion for others as the foundation of the "social contract.".

On the one hand, the political tradition of Hobbes saw human beings as driven by the natural right to self-preservation. Everything else fades in importance besides the need to survive. Humans do not do evil for their own sake but because it is necessary for survival. They imagine men in a natural world before society, in the free play of anarchy, when human beings face each other in a war of "all against all." According to Hobbes, his life in this state of nature was "solitary, poore, nasty, brutish and short." However, man also exhibits himself as a rational creature to pursue his self-interest, so humans entered into a social contract; each gives up some freedom to hurt or harm others to achieve greater freedom from fear. In this social contract, they agree to choose one from among him, and it doesn't matter who, as the Leviathan. Only the Leviathan has the power to kill and punish.

The States is the only one who possesses this right. The function of the Leviathan is to create conditions where human beings can freely compete while eliminating the feverish fear of others that surround them in their natural state. As my professor, H. Mark Roeloffs once said, man's life under the social contract is "solitary, poore, nasty, brutish, and slightly longer."

Freed from the fear of death, man can do what he wants as long as he does not harm others. "That principle is that the sole end for which humanity are warranted, individually or collectively, in interfering with the liberty of action of any of their number, is self-protection. That the only purpose for which power can be rightfully exercised over any member of a civilized community, against his will, is to prevent harm to others." "The individual is sovereign over himself and his own body and mind." (John Stuart Mill, On Liberty). "Of course, there is a vast difference between doing what one feels like doing while obeying the laws of the Leviathan and feelings of compassion, which play no part in the definition of freedom. Here, in Hobbes and Mill and other thinkers, we find life under capitalism pure and simple.

With Rousseau, and later in Marx, this truly self-serving view of man is posited against its opposite, that of compassion and empathy. This view of humanity is true not only of man but is universal in all living things: every living thing feels self-interest and compassion simultaneously. Jean Jacques tells us that a cow listening to another getting killed has this united feeling of self-interest and compassion as he moos and cries out for his fellows. Naked self-interest and compassion are the two components of a single unity, forming the foundation of Rousseau's Social Contract. Because we feel what others feel, there is a social contract, and there is a social contract because each person feels what others feel.

According to this definition, I am a sociopath. We are abnormal because we do not feel sympathy, empathy, or compassion for others; we do not feel as others feel. People like me, although avowing to the opposite view of humanity expressed by Rousseau and Marx, see the world only in terms of ourselves, our needs, our opinions, our status, and our power over others. Having little concern for anyone else, we proceed to a life of profound self-interest. The psychopath lives alone, and all his actions occur within this framework.

Within this context, he sees himself as superior to others. This feeling of innate superiority takes many and various forms. It may, for example, make others feel small to make yourself appear bigger. One way I did this was to criticize others, academically, socially, or in terms of my immediate family, to make myself seem superior. I sought only to make myself look good: my husbands, my children, other academics, and even occasionally, my students were victims of my criticism so that I might look good in relation to them. When my daughter Erica was a child, I took her to play miniature golf. Throughout the game, she was winning, but when I came to settle the final score, I cheated so that I would look good, and she would seem inferior. I would use my child to feel good about myself. My children, raised on constant criticism, were equally critical of their partners and children, and the pattern repeated. They rarely gave positive advice, focusing instead on what the people around them had done wrong.

Because I felt everyone was inferior to me, I had to dominate and control every conversation. I must conquer whether I was arguing with my spouse or lover, with my children, or in the context of an academic situation. My students adored this in me. I was fast and quick to respond, and my argument was flawless. However, I was only performing for the audience to admire me and give me the feeling of being superior to everyone.

Moreover, whenever I talked, I wanted to talk only about myself, about the moments in which I showed my superiority over others. I only wanted to hear about other people's needs on those occasions when I could use this as a means of manipulating them.

MEMORIES OF A PSYCHOPATH

It is always fascinating to pay attention to the way a psychopath speaks. For example, they do not use pronouns besides those that refer to them. They talk about themselves way more than other people. They seldom say the name of the person to whom they are speaking. They are conversing with themselves, and you are listening; there is no indication that what you have to say is important.

People not only existed so that they could hear about my life and not their own, but they also existed only in relation to my needs, wants, and desires. They are our servants, and no real or personal relationship can evolve between us aside from the relationship between servant and master, between superior and inferior. If we find someone, and we always do, who can serve and satisfy us, we are happy. Whether they are lovers or friends, immediate or extended family, they will perform this function until we are ready to cut them off, temporarily or permanently, until the time arises to have them serve us again or not. People have only use value to us. I have left behind a thousand people who have cared for me simply because they served no useful purpose.

For a person who views themselves as superior to others in every way, there is a great need to remain strong and independent. Psychopaths do not need others to survive. Very often, they will help others so that they will feel superior, but they never feel any need for the help of others except as servants for a particular need. For a person who views themselves as superior to others in every way, there is a great need to remain strong and independent. No matter how poor or needy I was, I would not ask anyone for help. Even when I could not afford it, I paid for dinners, gifts, and presents so that I would feel superior and not inferior.

Psychopaths do not dominate directly, and some do not- they rely on manipulating those around them. This manipulation takes the form of giving people the illusion that they are normal. I would rehearse the litany of feelings a natural person has to mimic them even though I never felt them. As a child living apart from my grandparents, I didn't know why other people behaved the way they did; I could see no correspondence between what they were thinking or feeling and how to interpret it. I did not know what I was expected to do if someone cried or if they were in pain. I had no show of empathy or compassion. I compensated for this by developing an array of emotions I could take out when needed. Emotions that made it seem that I felt what they felt when, in reality, I felt nothing. When I was young, I often got the feelings wrong; people would look at me because I had said something inappropriate about the situation. A woman came by with a baby, and I was pretty young, around 10, and I looked at it feeling nothing but knowing I had to say something. Instead of saying, "Isn't he cute or sweet," I said, "Oh, I want one just like it? The woman just looked at me.

Another time, I was playing outside with my friend, and we talked about what I would do if my parents died. I said to her that I would not care at all if my mother or stepfather died. She was in shock and went home and told her mother, who, in turn, told my mother, and I got in trouble for saying what I felt. But the fact was that I didn't care what happened to them.

Because of this tendency to hide what we are and to present ourselves as normal, psychopaths are also very good at lying. Other groups lie, to be sure, but psychopaths are particularly good at it. Either to individuals or to groups, they take great joy in telling untruths. I never did this because I felt compelled to tell others what was wrong with them or the system or something. I had no qualms about speaking the truth to anyone. But for others of my kind, if you are good at making another person think you are something you are not, then telling a lie is just a necessary part.

I behaved with indifference and cruelty. I remember when I was about 10, I was riding on the swings with my "friend" Johnny. It was quite a large swing, surrounded by parents watching their children. I got off the swing and stood with it in my hand. I saw Johnny riding back and forth. I watched for him to hit the peak of his swing, and then I let the swing go. I hit Johnny, and he fell to the floor and was bleeding very badly as the swing hit him just below the eye. I felt delighted when a young father came and comforted me. "It wasn't your fault; it was an accident," he told me. I just stood quietly looking at him and wondered what he was thinking to hold me innocent. I had done this deliberately, and I felt only a deep satisfaction for what I had done and no sense of guilt.

This cruelty manifested with anyone younger and more vulnerable to me: animals, children, or anyone I considered "inferior" to me. It extended to my husbands and lovers, except my first husband and my earliest lover, many years younger than me. I treated them all with a feeling of arrogance and control, belittling them in public and private. My sadism manifested itself in a constant barrage of insults to make the person feel smaller and inferior to me.

Ultimately, I did not want to be told how to change. I viewed every attempt at changing myself as the result of someone inferior telling me how to behave. Thus, a moment of relative insignificance can provoke unreasonable anger in which I hurled insults, yelled, and became physically abusive. At the slightest offense, I would go into a violent rage so intense that it was nearly impossible to control. My anger affected everyone in my life; no one was exempt. I was either quite pleasant to be with when things were going my way, and I appeared clever, charismatic, and charming to everyone, or in a violent rage because things were not going my way. It would be even worse if, at any point, I felt I was being disrespected or disregarded. I never killed anyone because of the social contract I lived under, but I wanted to. The fear of the Leviathan hung over me and kept me in check.

When I was not enraged, I was exceedingly charismatic. I held everyone in awe, mainly because I was so intelligent. My students thought I spoke with an almost magical feel to my words: a feeling of enchantment and hypnosis. One of the psychiatrists speaking on Adolf

Hitler said the following: "He became "extremely animated." You have this contrast between a "person who is internally empty, and somebody who gets on stage, and stands before a microphone and pours out words, the ultimate charismatic prophet that people just go wild about. The basis of charisma is the charismatic figure and the charismatic audience." This was not true. There are leaders, and there are followers; it is because a leader gives the impression of leading that he has an audience who is more than willing to follow him. It is what made me long to be a teacher; I spoke and held my students in a charismatic embrace with me. I lived for this; it was the most essential part of my life. If I had been born a male with the same sense of privilege as that male, I would have exceeded Adolf Hitler in my ability to move people.

We tend to be extremely intelligent, as I once was in my heyday. But aside from being charismatic and thoughtful, we also suffer flaws that frustrate and fluster us. These include "poor judgment and failure to learn from experience, pathological egocentricity and incapacity for love, lack of remorse or shame, impulsivity, grandiose sense of self-worth, pathological lying, manipulative behavior, poor self-control, promiscuous sexual behavior, juvenile delinquency, and criminal versatility among others." I suffered from all of these, except juvenile and adult crimes. Again, the Leviathan stood in my way.

Even when I was too young to be self-aware, I understood things. By this, I mean not material possessions but the traits of character that accompany any drive toward self-fulfillment typical of a narcissist and sadist, and not people, were what was important to me. I dreamed of glory, fame, recognition before the masses, and a way of asserting my power and superiority. I dreamed of existing at the galaxy's center, surrounded by those I could use to help me achieve these dreams. This dream was so important to me that I would leave everything behind to fulfill it. But when I was too young to understand, I was beginning to express the outlook of my existence as a narcissistic, sadistic psychopath. Even though the lack of awareness is not fully present, the impulses are.

If the need for change does enter our frame of reference, or if we do, for some reason, doubt our superiority, there is the possibility with me and with other psychopaths that we sink into a depression and see ourselves as hopeless, as the opposite of who we are, not superior but inferior to those to those who have a normal feeling for life. This tells us what we already know- that our lives are meaningless to the lives of others we denigrate. We blame ourselves and suffer self-hatred as the product of our unresolved conflicts. We are miserable.

Chapter 3: Memories of My Childhood

I am in Bishkek, Kyrgyzstan, on Christmas Eve as I sit to write this. I smell coal everywhere, for Bishkek is heated not by oil but by coal, and a hazy smog fills the air. It burned my eyes and gave me a sore throat when I woke up in the morning, and I coughed incessantly, but at the same time, the smell of coal entered my consciousness and carried me back to the town in which I grew up, to Nanticoke, Pennsylvania, and the early memories of my life there.

My world revolved around coal for the first eight years of my life. To be sure, we burned a higher grade of coal, Anthracite, and not Bituminous, which did not offend the bronchial passages as much as that in Bishkek. Anthracite has a high carbon content, making it extremely hard to burn. As a result, it burns slowly and without producing much smoke. It is one step closer to being pure diamonds and did not offend the mucous membranes as much. My grandfather was an Anthracite coal miner there and went into the mines daily to support his family until he could no longer.

When I was old enough, I wandered through the slag heaps, helping my grandmother pick up loose coal to feed the coal stove on which we depended for heat and cooking. Having no other source of entertainment, no radio or television as I didn't understand English, we sat on frigid winter evenings around the open grate. We listened to my family's stories about the old country and life in the new. Our lives, every part of it, was somehow centered on coal, and that coal stove on which we were so dependent for heat, cooking, light, and entertainment was the centerpiece of my life.

The love of gambling runs deep in my family. One of my Mongolian ancestors from Lida, Belarus, lost his entire estate on the turn of a card and immediately drowned himself in the pond on the property. We bet on the horses, we bet on the numbers, we bet on everything we could, and we loved to play poker. Every weekend, we would get together with serious gamblers and play. It was the mark of my womanhood when as a teenager, I was invited to play poker with them.

No accident then that my mother, who had just gotten out of the hospital with me, should not wait long for her fix. I was approximately one month old when she asked my aunts, Eva, and Bertha, if they would come and watch me while she went out to play a few hands of poker. My Mother was nursing me, and they expected her to return in time to feed me. But one hour led to the next; one day became another, and she did not return. In desperation, my aunts, who could not find my mother at any of the games, heated a bottle of milk and gave it to me. Having drunk it, I slept for the whole day. But I cried for a long time, and whether or not this factor shaped my personality, I don't know.

By the second day, my Aunt Bertha decided to call my grandmother in Pennsylvania. She was there when my mother returned. She told her she was taking me because my mother was irresponsible. My Grandmother is formidable, and almost no one dared argue with her. My Mother responded, "You will see how difficult she is to raise and bring her back." I was a very hard child to take care of. I was born with an easily irritated personality, a hint of what would come. But my grandmother didn't bring me back. She had infinite patience, especially for her only grandchild. I went to live with her in Nanticoke, Pennsylvania.

The homes the miners lived in, the food they bought, and whatever they needed were purchased from the company. They were doing little more than working for their sustenance. My Grandmother was clever enough to know she had to get out from under the mine owner's influence. She lived a very frugal life, a habit that stuck with me. She picked mushrooms and berries from the surrounding woods. She grew potatoes, tomatoes, and beets in her garden. We lived off of potatoes three times a day: mashed potatoes, boiled potatoes, fried potatoes, and my absolute favorite, potato pancakes. We ate borsht without meat. We picked the cabbage and pickled it to make a massive barrel of Kapustka, or fermented cabbage. When we did have meat, she made Kielbasa out of it and hung them over the coal stove over the kitchen to dry. She kept chickens and rabbits. I could never say I wanted for anything as my grandmother's food was enough. I did not envy anyone.

But my grandmother had another gift: the ability to interpret dreams. She inherited this from her mother, who lived in Belarus, and it went from generation to generation in her family. We lived in a world in which most people did not speak English. They came from the "old country" and could not listen to the radio to discover what was happening. There was no television. These people lived in ignorance, so the interpretation of dreams was their only way to understand what was happening in their lives.

We were like the ancient Greeks, who went to Oracles to decide what was happening because they could not interpret the world. The Greek women were chosen by the gods who knew how to give divine advice. My Grandmother functioned as an oracle who interpreted life for the people around her. Mary would listen to these dreams and tell the people what they meant. She was so good at it that people came to her from all over Luzerne County to have her interpret their dreams and advise them on what they should do. She was the Oracle at Nanticoke.

My Grandmother bought a cow through her frugality and ability to interpret dreams. She got milk for her children and the ability to make cheese from the cow. She would take the cheese to stores that would buy them. It was just a matter of time before my grandmother put her money down on the house, and we were out of the company town. She bought a small single-story house and then divided it so that one half was ours and somebody rented out the other half. In that small house, she raised her children; when they were grown, she also introduced me. I lived in that tiny house with my grandmother, Mary, and my grandfather, Valentine. I slept in the same bed with them until I was almost 7.

Valentine, by then, was nearing the end of his days as a coal miner. He worked for a few years, but he got "coal miner asthma," which resulted from breathing in coal for all the days of his life. Its more formal name was pneumoconiosis, and many who worked with him developed it because of their exposure to airborne dust. Pneumoconiosis had no cure.

I watched him die without knowing what death was. He was always very gentle with me. He put up with my tantrums. When he could not take me fishing with him one Saturday because he was so ill, he offered me a lollipop as a bribe. I threw a tantrum, and all the while I was doing so, I looked at his eyes, how sad and disappointed they were, and felt guilt for what I was doing.

But soon, he could not go anywhere with me anymore. He sat at the foot of the stove and drank his Scotch whiskey heated on the coal. I spent lots of time with him then, talking and playing games and listening to his heartbeat. I understood that he was not dead as long as it was beating, yet I knew nothing about death or dying. Soon, he went into the hospital. He came home absolutely delighted with hospital food. He began to insist that my grandmother, who knew nothing about such things, go out to get "cornflakes," which was a taste he had acquired in the hospital.

Yet, all the while, I continued to throw my tantrums at the old man. I asked him once if he could draw a picture of the cross on the side of the kitchen. He drew a small cross, not the "picture" I wanted. I threw a tantrum. My grandparents, who could not read or write, were at a disadvantage because they could not help me with my homework when I started school. One day, I needed to learn a poem for the holidays, but I could not and threw a tantrum. I told my grandparents that when I grew up, I would learn to read and never stop. It has been a promise I have always kept.

MEMORIES OF A PSYCHOPATH

One particular aspect of my personality was that I was somehow a "blessed" child. My grandfather would leave packages of candies at the front door. When I saw them on my way out, my grandmother would proclaim that they were God-given gifts. How lucky I was to get gifts from God. Then there was the candy store owner, who my grandfather told to give me what I wanted, and he would pay the cost. All of these things contributed to my narcissism, so as the chosen child of God who got everything, I wanted without having to pay for it. It was mine because I deserved it.

I want you to understand that this did not mean I got everything, but rather that I wished for so little and got it. We were a poor family, and I had no wish other than for the things I wanted. My Grandmother's cooking, the candy I got from God, and the ice cream I got from the store; the horses my grandmother gave me so I could play Cowboys and Indians. I had no desire for anything else; there was no car I envied, no clothing I needed, no toys or trinkets I desired. There was no TV to inspire me to want such things, so they never entered my consciousness.

On top of this, I was paranoid. One Christmas Eve, I sat listening to my aunt's talking about something I could not understand because I did not understand English very well, being seeped in my grandmother's language. I kept watching them spell the word "ball" and then look at me. I ran to my grandmother and told her what they had done, that they said this word and looked at me. She, believing everything I said, went downstairs and told my aunts they had to leave. Of course, no one argued with my grandmother, and they went off, in the middle of the night, to Jersey City.

In First Grade we had been given small coin box, one of those things that you put coins into and then brought it back to school. I ran away and hid until my aunts went looking for me and found me hidden under a car. They asked me what was wrong, and I told them I would not get money to put me into one of those "iron lungs" for sick children. My family laughed, but the fact remained that I was becoming paranoid because I did not understand English, and so I thought that everyone was talking about me. It went away to a large degree after I learned English, but it never entirely left me, and I am still a paranoid person.

My Grandmother was also very kind to me but in a different way. When I first lived with her, she took me to visit one of her secret foes. She was a woman who told fortunes, which were very popular and famous. It was a big deal for her to take me because this was someone to whom she hardly spoke. But she took me, and the woman let her in. My Grandmother asked her what my life would be like. The woman said I would be alone as it would be my destiny. No matter what, I would find myself alone. My Grandmother accepted this as if it were a fact of life and began raising me as if I were alone. Mary told me not to turn to anyone for my physical comfort. When I would fall, she taught me how to get up without relying on anyone for consolation. She would watch me climb a tree and then watch me fall, and her only words of comfort to me were to tell me to get up.

I remember one occasion when I believed I dreamed I could fly. I so thought it that when I woke up, I went and stood at the steps down to the kitchen and said to her, "Baba, look, I can fly," and I hurled myself off the staircase. I thought I had broken my back when I landed from the fall. The pain was unbearable. My Grandmother turned and looked at me, never offering me any help. She said, "So, do you think you can fly?" And I told her, "No, I can't fly." And she waited for me to get up off the floor. It wasn't easy, but I could walk, which meant I was okay for her and me. I would not be a person who felt my every need should be fulfilled. I was tough, and I was strong.

She gave me endless lectures as well. She taught me, for example, never to believe anything someone told me but rather to find out for myself. "If you ask someone something, they will lie to you. You have to go and find out things for yourself." She gave me the example of how she often got the wrong ones when she asked for directions because the people telling her lied to her. As a result, I learned I had to find out things for myself, which set the tone for my scholarship.

She taught me, as well, how to distrust everyone. She was, without question, a hateful woman. More appropriately, Mary was a woman who hated everyone to whom she wasn't related and, sometimes, those to whom she was related. This was a direct result of her being a young woman in a foreign country, but it was also a part of her. Mary fought with everyone, and it made me, in so far as I imitated her, a fighter as well. It enjoyed it and winning was the only thing that mattered. She fought with her husband even though he was violent with her. She fought with her children when they annoyed her. Her favorite was my aunt, Bertha, who was dark in complexion relative to the rest of my family. My grandmother would call her a "black bastard" and tell her she adopted her. This statement would send my aunt into fits of crying, and my grandmother would be satisfied. When she was older, she put things in my Aunt Berta's bed which she would feel when sleeping, all the while denying she had done so. This trait in my grandmother and me was a throwback to our ancient Mongol relatives, to Jebe, who lived to fight with warring tribes. I never really learned how to get along with anyone, and if I did, it was merely a way of making peace until I could fight with them again.

She was always there. Sometimes, on those rare occasions where I was allowed to play with others, I would see her standing behind a tree watching me. She was always close by, and I felt cared for and protected, knowing that if somebody did something to me, she would emerge and make it right. I felt, at least for part of my childhood, cared for and protected. For a long time after she was gone, when the hint of something terrible came to me, I used to pray to her to make it better. After a while, I stopped.

Chapter 4: Memories of My Self

Catholics claim that Loyola said that if you gave him the child when it was born, he would give you back the man when he was seven, the age of reason and, hence, the age of Communion. However, it was Aristotle who said this first, and Loyola who followed him, for it was not just the Jesuits but the Franciscans and the Dominicans who were dedicated Aristotelians. St. Thomas Aquinas, a devout Dominican himself, became so fascinated with the newly found philosophy of Aristotle that he built the dogma of the church around it. Aquinas, who began teaching at the University of Paris in 1252, saw that all university students master Aristotle to receive a university decree. Dominican defenders of his teaching assured a victory for the cause of Christian Aristotelianism, which became known as Scholasticism. It continued to exert significant influence until the Renaissance and Reformation, when a reaction against Aristotle occurred throughout Europe. From the fourteenth to the eighteenth centuries, the humanist and scientific movements left Aristotelianism aside in favor of newer approaches to thought.

Yet, in this modern age of scientific thinking, we find the ideas of Aristotle about raising children are still valid; the formation of a child takes place in the early years of life and remains fixed from then on. It is the attachment to the primary caregiver that sets the prototype for all future social relations. On this basis, it enables individuals to predict, control, and manipulate interaction with others, giving us a very early glimpse into the man. By the age of 7, I was formed into being what I was, and no matter what experience I engaged in after that point, I remained a psychopath. The adventures of the rest of my life, which differed from their beginnings, accumulated on me as a psychopath, making me more, not less, than I was.

I was an extremely high-strung child; perhaps because I was not fed as a young child or probably because I was born that way, I don't know. As a result of the way my grandmother raised me, I believed I was superior to everyone else. After all, God gave me candy, and all I had to do was ask for something at the candy store, and I got it. There was nothing more important to me than candy.

I was the chosen child of my grandparents and Aunt Berth and Aunt Eva, all of whom spoiled me. If I didn't get what I wanted, I threw a tantrum until I did. I want you to understand that this did not mean that I got everything and anything, but instead that I wanted so little and got it. We were a poor family, and I had no wish other than for the things I liked: my grandmother's cooking, the candy I got from God, the ice cream I got from the store, the "horses" my grandmother gave me so I could play cowboys and Indians. I had no desire for anything else, no car I envied, no clothing I needed, no toys or trinkets I desired. There was no TV to inspire me to want such things, so they never entered my consciousness.

Coming out of the war had also shaped me. My family's pride in participating in the war and the fact that I belonged to the winning country made me feel I was a victor and not a victim. In this context, I saw myself as someone who fought a war against the Nazis and won.

In the world of my grandmother, I was in a constant battle against those I did not know or trust. When she fought with the woman next door, or her archenemy, the woman who foretold people's fortunes, or any other enemies she found, I felt proud of her rather than guilty because she failed to get along with people. In the war of "all against all," I was a winner and felt superior.

As my destiny was to be alone, I learned never to rely on anyone but to care for myself and be independent. I might wine if I didn't get what I wanted, but I never cried if I got hurt. Throughout it all, I felt strong. When this idyllic childhood was left behind, when my grandfather finally gave way to death, I was ready to endure. It didn't matter what anyone did to me, for being given childhood by those who raised me, especially my grandmother, I was at seven, ready for my psychopathic life.

I was sent to Jersey City for a few days. When I returned home, I ran upstairs to see my grandfather resting. I jumped on him and discovered he was cold. "Why is he so cold, Baba, I asked." "He went fishing and fell in the water, that is why." But, of course, I did not understand that he had died. His death was the one factor that changed my life forever. It did not change me, but it changed the circumstances under which I came to live.

When I realized he had gone, I went into the fields and tried to kill myself by jumping into the reservoir. But I couldn't do it, and so I returned home. I remember the funeral. My Grandmother tried to throw herself into the coffin. I remember the dinner afterward when I watched everyone eating, drinking, and having a good time. It seemed so strange that they were so happy, and my grandfather was dead. That was the point at which his death faced me as a reality.

I know I begged my grandmother not to sell the house she lived in and move to Jersey City, but she did anyway. In time, I understood that I would live with my mother, her new husband, and my sister, who was just born. I didn't understand any of it because nothing was explained to me. I was just taken, against my will, so to speak, and brought into this world without any discussion. Nobody asked me what I wanted.

I went to live in the Horseshoe section of New Jersey, in an old "project" close to where Frank Hague, the Mayor of Jersey City, had grown up when he was a child. There were no woods to go searching for mushrooms and berries, no garden for me to roam in; there were no cowboys and Indians to play with my friends. My horse, Lackatoria, was left behind with the memories of my childhood. And so, I began the most horrible existence of my life, living with my mother.

My Mother, who had a baby, spent most of her time sleeping, and when she was awake, she ignored me. My aunts and uncles who visited us very often did not come by. And my grandmother, on whom I was so dependent and who I loved, rarely came to see me. We lived in an apartment heated by oil, so I had no coal stove to gather around and listen to my family. I felt abandoned and, yes, alone.

I had initially felt this way deeply but not consciously when I was taken away from my mother. I did not have any sensibility of it, but I thought myself lost without her. My father, too, was gone from me as well. I don't know where he was or what happened to him. We never spoke about him when I was a child. It didn't matter whether they were good or bad; the fact was they were my mother and father, and being taken from them meant that I was, without knowing it, depressed. I felt this loneliness until I had my daughter, Tiel. I woke up the next day, and I was no longer lonely but felt that I belonged to her and she to me. Tiel was the end of that loneliness that haunted me all of my life but which I did not recognize. But this was the mother of my birth and not the Mother I returned to after all my years with my grandparents. I had no feelings at all for my mother.

When my grandmother did come by for a few moments, I would beg her to stay. At one point, I clung to her jacket and made her sit near my bed so she would be there in the morning. When I awoke, she was gone, and I still held her jacket as if my life depended on it. I knew then that she was gone forever. That the woman I had loved so dearly in my life was no more and that only the outer feeling of her, her semblance, was what I had left. There was no one to cling to, and I was, in the most profound sense of the word, what the Old Woman said I would be - alone.

Chapter 5: Memories of Realizations

My mother, who thought I should get an excellent Catholic education, sent me to St. Lucy's school. If the events of my life were horrifying, this was the most frightening. From the nuns, I would learn that the things I cherished were not provided for free or out of the goodness of God but had a value and the power of corporal punishment I had never experienced before. The nuns were forever hitting us with rulers. I, who had never been hit or disciplined, was now the constant object of abuse.

Sometimes, when a male child was bad, he would be called to the front of the class and sent under the desk. The nun would then sit down and smile as he moved around. When they misbehaved, the boys were sent to the principal's office for their punishments. When they returned, they couldn't walk. I was glad I was a girl and only got punished by being hit on my hands with a ruler.

Finally, there was the sale of the candies, which profoundly influenced me. I used to get candies from God and the storeowner, who let me have whatever I wanted. I learned that candies did not come from God or the store owner but were bought from the nuns. My favorites were shaped like mint leaves and tasted like spearmint. But I never had a penny to spend on candies because my mother never gave me any money. So, the children who had money bought the sweets, and the others, like me, sat there and watched the other children eat them. I craved those candies so badly and learned from this experience the power of money to get what I wanted.

I had not learned to read. I had yet to learn to speak English properly. But I found the solution to my problem in the neighbor next door. He would sit with me every day, and I can't remember what he taught me, but somehow, I learned how to read. I am forever grateful to this man, even though I don't know his name. I learned English as I went through school. And in time, I became what I promised my

Grandmother I would; I became a lover of books. But this was after my great obsession with television.

I was somewhere near eight when I first watched TV. We had one brought to my house, and while my mother slept, I began to watch it. I really couldn't figure out why anyone would do anything but watch TV. There were comedies like I Love Lucy. There were cowboys and Indians, oh my God. There was entertainment, like watching the Ed Sullivan show. And it kept me so busy, so occupied that I could deal with the rest of my life.

But still, problems began to emerge from this trying time. I began to walk on my toes. My mother hardly noticed, but I found out later that it was a sign of depression. I became so ill with an infection in my right knee that it swelled up to twice its size. My Grandmother taught me never to complain, so I endured it. But it got so bad that my mother, who likewise ignored it, took me to the hospital, where I got antibiotics. My mother also seldom fed me, so I spent much time eating mayonnaise and bread. My mother was not my grandmother who prepared breakfast, lunch, and dinner for me and gave me candies and ice cream. She was a woman who ignored me. When she did feed me, it was a trauma. One of the things she loved to make was split pea soup. I hated it. When she put it down in front of me, I just said to her that I wouldn't eat it and started to leave the table. She slapped me across the face, and I, in turn, slapped her. I had never been hit before. It went on like this until I gave up. When we studied catechism, her way of dealing with me was to hit me for every mistake I made. She smacked me so many times that my wrists were swollen at the end of the session, but I never cried out or complained. She made my life hell for the short time she gave me. I was a spoiled child and needed discipline to stop throwing my tantrums, but it was too late. Aristotle was right. I did not give in and put up with her abuse, so she was frustrated because she could not change me. I don't remember ever crying.

Fortunately, her basic tendency was to sleep or to go out and play poker, so she left me alone, and I was happy to be alone with the TV to watch. I lived in a world of fantasies, and it was beautiful. I couldn't understand why anyone would do anything but watch TV.

Sometimes, though, she let me out of the house. When it was hot, she let me play in the sprinklers, which was a new experience. It was the first time I was around people of color, and I thought it was terrible that people let themselves get so dirty. But when I saw them running through the sprinklers and coming out just as dirty as they went in, I realized they were a different color than me. There was no sign of prejudice, as I had grown up in a white world, and this was simply something different from what I was used to. But I always played alone. I had no friends, nor did I want any. The children were strange to me, and I, in turn, felt odd in relation to them. My Grandmother had taught me to stay away from all children except those she felt were suitable. Now, there was no grandmother to decide who was appropriate and who was not.

There was one experience I can't quite explain to you. It was nearly Fall, and I went and sat on the bench and watched the people. An older man, perhaps around 60, came and sat beside me. In a few minutes, he asked me, "Does a cat have whiskers?" And I did not know I did not. I said no, and he responded, without looking at me, that a cat does have whiskers. Then he asked me if a dog had whiskers, and I said no. He responded that a dog does have whiskers. But in the very essence of that conversation, I met someone who taught me how profoundly ignorant I was. This man, who had no idea what he was doing, took on the role of teacher to me. And I, who did not know the answer to his questions, had to find out. He and the older man across the hall were my first teachers. I considered them as such.

My stepfather, Louis Biesiada, came up on weekends. During the week, he was building our house on the Jersey Shore. I was indifferent to my sister. I remained so all of my life. She was someone who, by her very existence, forced me into this situation I found unbearable. I could not relate to her as my sister, a family member, because I had no family to connect to then. I was so busy trying to stay alive in this horrible circumstance that was so different from my past when my grandfather was alive.

Soon, we were to move from here to the place my stepfather had built on the Jersey Shore. My world changed for the better because I was no longer cooped up in an apartment with my mother. The ocean was beautiful and wild, and I only had to worry about the snapping turtles everywhere. We would have huge cookouts with my stepfather's friends out on the shore of the beach, and the ocean was a never-ending comfort to me. I took to the habit of running along the beach almost every day, and as a result, I developed strong legs. I learned to fish from my stepfather and did so most evenings. Sometimes, we went out in the boat, where I discovered I was seasick. The men, not wanting to go back, just threw me overboard, and I learned to be a good swimmer.

In time, I made friends from the neighborhood. They were all males, and so I began to play sports. I found I had incredible instincts; I could tell where the ball was going once it was hit and could catch it. I played basketball and football. I would have been encouraged to be an athlete if I had lived during another time and not the fifties.

It was fine while I was young, but as soon as I started to get older, my mother and I had a serious discussion as my menstruation started. She cried when she told me everyone said I was a "Tom Boy." She told me she would kill me if I were one of them. I didn't quite understand what she was saying, although I do now. My mother said that she wanted me to be more of a lady, more feminine. When my mother finished, I leaned over and told her that I had no intention of being a lady or the kind of woman she wanted me to be. There was nothing she could do, really, nothing. And she knew it, and she left me alone. We had our discussion, and it was over, and I wasn't going to change myself to suit her. I loved sports.

And yes, there was a heavy price paid for being athletic. My love of sports meant that I was not a woman to be desired. I did not have boyfriends, and I did not date. I did not attend one dance in high school. Moreover, I wore no makeup and kept my hair short, as I do now. There were boys I was attracted to. One of them was the son of the Principal of the High School. His smile captured me, and I thought he could do great things. I adored him for a long time. However, when I saw the girl, he was going with and how feminine and helpless she was, I envied her for being attractive to him, but I was unwilling to change myself to become her. I would rather be alone than give up the things I loved: my sports and my growing scholarly involvement. Later, when I got older, it didn't matter much. Men, or at least some men, were very attracted to me, and it didn't matter whether I was an athlete and a scholar or a woman who didn't wear makeup. But at this point, it mattered, and still, I was set in my ways

Chapter 6: Memories of My Mother

For a long time, though, she played Mother most of the years from 9 through 12. She cooked, although it was very bad. She kept her house clean, which was terrific as the sand from the ocean came in everywhere.

Her favorite task was ironing, which she did with a passion. It was her way of relaxing. Sometimes, I used to get up in the middle of the night only to find her ironing at two or three a.m.

She belonged to a Catholic organization run by Mrs. Slowinski, who used old clothing to make bandages for cancer patients. She would go once a week to make bandages. But things began to fall apart for her. They discovered she had been a married woman before she married my father. She had a Catholic marriage and so could not get married again. This sin ended her relationship with the Church.

As for her marriage, her husband needed to make more money for us to get by. It wasn't that he didn't try, for he did. It was that the people whom he did business with were just a little cleverer, and so he gave wrong estimates and lost money. At other times, they didn't do the work through no fault of his own, and he had to work for no salary. It was all a matter of poor administration. He compensated for this by drinking, and when he drank and came home late for dinner, her wife response was to fight with him.

The whole relationship started to deteriorate. Soon, to survive, my mother had to go to work. Louis was naturally a little upset about this as, in the 1950s, a man who could not support his family was considered a failure. She went to work, and I found myself absolutely alone. I was totally at a loss, as, of course, no one told me. I sat around and sat around, and finally, I decided I would also go to work.

The man who lived next door had a business owning and supplying gumball machines. Part of what he did was to take a bunch of toys he got from overseas, place them in plastic containers, and then put them in dispensing machines. I went to ask him if I could do this, and he said yes, so I began working and making money. I, at last, had a few pennies to call my own.

As my mother began working and we began to save some money, the marriage continued deteriorating. He drank more, and so too did she. At first, it was only a tiny amount; a glass of sherry was taken in the afternoon, then it became two, and then it was no longer sherry but wine. Then, it was hard liquor. In my mother's old age, she developed alcoholism.

She also began to spend some time playing "bingo." We still played poker every weekend we could, but this became her new passion. She would go once or twice a week and play. Over the course of her bingo playing, she found a boyfriend, and my job became one of hiding it from my stepfather. Of course, her boyfriend was married, and the results were that my stepfather and his wife knew. His wife once asked me whether I was ashamed of what my mother did. I said no. I felt no shame for what my mother did.

Nor did she stop there. There was another boyfriend after this one, another married man. It continued for a long time, but he didn't leave his wife. She was drinking heavily now, and if I wanted to find her, I didn't go home but to the local bar called Murphy's, where she was drinking Rob Roy's and flirting with the guys. She always went to work. She worked as a waitress for a long time at the Cozy Nook and made good money. But she was done with the whole housewife number, and I ate most of my meals out and spent a lot of my time alone.

The remarkable hold that television had on me was ended by my days at the Jersey Shore. The salt buildup on the antennae, and if we had any reception, it was so poor. In any case, I stopped watching TV and began reading. I read and reread Sir Arthur Conan Doyle's stories of Sherlock Holmes. I soon acquired the ability to look at things and observe what they reveal to us, and in the case of the Hound of Baskerville, what they did not reveal, I read the classics. I was utterly taken by how Tom Sawyer used his wits to have his other friends whitewash his fence. I lost myself in books as it was the only escape from reality besides my work.

But in general, all the reading did not help me with school. I was considered, and I considered myself to be stupid. I was poor in math, miserable in history, and awful in science. The only thing I was good at was gym. The school and I were both waiting for me to turn sixteen so I could go out into the world and get a job in a factory. But all that was to change.

To begin with, I enrolled in a class called Journalism. It was too advanced for me, and I am trying to figure out how or why the school allowed me to register, but I did. Whatever the reason, I came alive intellectually with this course, and my natural ability to write began to express itself. The teacher of that class, Dr. Martin, had a PhD, so the school was fortunate to have him. He was around 40, with a balding head and a great sense of humor. I fell in love with him. I thought of him day and night and talked about him every chance I could get. I collected small secrets regarding his childhood and early life, which I kept in notebooks. I lived my life so he would appreciate me, and I, in turn, was appreciated. He was my Father, someone who cared for and cared for me and cared about what I did. I was one of the most outstanding writers in the class.

I came alive not just in writing but in art as well. My teacher had trained at the Philadelphia Museum College of Art and was a wizard at teaching. My artistic ability improved, and I was selected twice to teach the class when students were chosen to be the teacher for one day. I knew then what I had known all along that I desperately wanted to be a teacher. I wasn't sure what kind of teacher I wanted to be, but I felt the need to teach to express my growing need to be important in the world.

There was another occasion in which I came to understand myself. The principal called me in to speak to me. I had no idea why and thought that perhaps I had gotten into trouble. He told me the school had given its annual high school IQ test, and he was astounded by the fact that I had the school's highest IQ. He was a little perplexed because, at this point, he was hoping that I would quit at 16. But there was no way I was leaving; I had found my niche in life. I was going to be somebody; I was going to assert my ego.

I started writing poetry and got much of it published in the high school journal. I became a select AWK club member, whose only life task was to be quite intellectual. I was a member of the art club that helped decorate the school for occasions like Christmas and Halloween. There was no end to my glory when I finally "found" myself.

Over time, I went to work at Murphy's as his daughter was a friend of mine. I started off working as a salad chef. The place had a huge business, and I chopped salads and put them into bins so the waitpersons could gather them for dinner. Very soon after that, the chef's wife, who also worked there, was to have trouble with her pregnancy. And I got promoted to second chef and worked there every summer after that. I was a second chef, and I knew everything a chef had to do to make it work. I frequently worked 50 to 60 hours a week, but I made great money. As I recall, I made over 400 dollars a week. My Mother, who was so concerned that I saved my money, told me to give it to her and she would put it in the bank. I did as I was saving money to go to college. When I went to ask her for the money, she told me she had used it to pay the mortgage. I didn't say a word. I was going to college, and if I were lucky, I would never return to my mother's house again. Or so I thought.

Chapter 7: Memories of Keuka College

I got a scholarship to study art, and that, combined with a work program, enabled me to attend Keuka College. I worked most days at the college cafeteria, which was great because I had extra access to the food. The chef was Polish, and his cooking was fantastic. I had run a kitchen in my younger days as a chef, but here, I was confined to dishwashing. I didn't mind as work was work. I also began to work at the local coffee shop a few days a week. I was busy working, and I was sleeping the rest of the time. I did not do a lot of studying.

I was sleeping not because I missed home but because I could not figure out how to get along with the people around me. I felt as if I lived in one world and they, meaning everyone else, lived in another. I did not understand why they were being so warm and civil. I didn't understand people's thinking because I didn't understand their motivations.

I was still a poor student who cared nothing about math or science, but my writing was exceptional, and it carried me through, at least until I met Lotus Snow. I did not understand why my writing bothered her, but now, considerably later, I know. Early in the semester, I was assigned to an English teacher for the year. However, we were introduced to the faculty early in the year. It was during that meeting that I met Professor Lotus Snow. She was about 50 years old. She wore thick glasses that enlarged her eyes and made it seem like she focused on you alone when she spoke to you. She kept staring at me the whole meeting. Finally, she came over and asked if I wanted to be in her class.

Of course, I was flattered and said yes; she recognized my inherent superiority. I immediately changed my classes and looked forward to writing for her. My first essay was an analysis of Hedda Gabler. It was truly brilliant, and my mastery of the English language manifested itself everywhere. However, it shocked my system when the essay I gave her came back with an F-. I went to ask her why. Dr. Snow looked at me with that strange look and told me that if I wanted to discuss it, I should visit her in her apartment. "But I am here," I answered. "Why can't we discuss it here?" "Come to my apartment," she said. I did not go and got more bad marks for my writing. I was devastated. I never got an explanation but was told to come to her apartment, and we would discuss it. I, of course, did not realize she was gay.

Meanwhile, I was in a strange group, even by my standards. There was this woman who behaved as if she were a gang member. She walked around telling people what to do and threatening them. I avoided her as much as possible, but we soon were on our way to a confrontation; with my easily frustrated self, I soon lost my temper with her and, with it, my fear of her.

She had developed a relationship with my roommate, which meant she could enter the room any time she wanted, turn on the lights, wake up my roommate, play cards, or have a conversation. It didn't matter to her what time this was. To be sure, we had places where she could go and have a conversation, but she decided to do it this way. Of course, I was asleep. Mostly, I just ignored her because I was a heavy sleeper. But on this one occasion, I could not, so I told her to go into the other room. She told me to go "fuck myself." I lost control, stood up, and said to her that if she didn't get out of there right now, there would be a price to pay. She looked at me and kept right on talking. I jumped on her, and we began to fight, and she was losing. She ran out of the room, and my roommate's response was to ask me how I could do something like that to her and run after her. She never came into the room again, but I broke my relationship with my roommate and didn't care. I was content to be by myself.

There was another woman who lived across the hall from me called Dixie Dibble. I wonder whether that was her real name or an assumed name under which she wrote, for she was an author who specialized in cowboy stories. Her chief protagonist was Jingle Bob Jones. Even though she had grown up in Long Island, she was Jingle Bob. She wore

Western gear, fancy shirts, and cowboy boots and talked with a twang. I read one of the Jingle Bob Jones novels at her request, for she had written several dozens of these and could not believe how bad it was. She tried to get them published but has yet to do so. But there is no question that she was living out the character of Jingle Bob in her personality. She was Jingle Bob Jones. She was also a close friend of Lotus Snow's. Not knowing anything about Lesbians, I didn't think for one moment that either she or Lotus were Lesbians. But, of course, they were. They were lovers.

My artistic ability was also suffering. One professor thought I should offer a lot of touch and feel in my paintings. He didn't know much of what I was doing. The other professor, William Best, was a technician. When I started to paint, he asked me whether I was using hard or cold-pressed oils. I didn't know, so I had to stop and find out the difference. He taught me much about painting, particularly his art, which relied on Meyer's Medium. It gave a ghostly glow to his subjects. Wonderful. But I wasn't focusing on anything as I was so depressed and did not understand why.

I became friends with a brilliant woman named Dee Deque. She was exceptionally tall, blond, and tended to put on weight. She lived not far from Lake Keuka in Sodus Point, and I would go with her to one of her many parties. They were, for me, what parties always are: an opportunity to meet other people and practice the emotions I felt without experiencing them, for I was still very young and did not know how to respond to people's feelings. About mid-way through the first semester, Dee quit school and moved to New York. In time, she asked me to join her. At first, it was just for visits, but over time, permanently, before I got my first apartment.

All of this ended somewhere toward the end of my first year. I was sleeping too much. I had barely gotten by with my school performance. I fought with my roommate's girlfriends. The fight didn't bother me, but it did make people a little wary of me. I spent a lot of time mocking

Dixie Dibble to my friends, which was ever so easy to do and made me feel superior. I was forever failing when it came to Lotus Snow's class. Next, it would be time for the Police to come and visit me.

But first, I had gotten involved with a local guy. He had gone to Rensselaer Polytechnic University but quit or flunked out. I got involved with him mainly because he would sneak me off campus in his car. I would sign out as if I were going to the library, and then he would meet me nearby. We went out to dinner or parties or, if his mother was out, we had sex, although the sex didn't mean much to him or me. I was asexual at that point. It was just a way to get off campus and away from it all.

The dean called me to her office, and when I was there, she left. In a few minutes, the Police came. To put it bluntly, they accused me of planning an attack on Dixie Dibble. She had been attacked all those times I had signed out for the library. Someone had thrown a stone at her from the cliff above the river. She claimed she was attacked by someone who tried to push her into the water from a cliff. I looked at them, not knowing what to say. If I said that I had been with my boyfriend, it was the equivalent of being thrown out of school, as we were never allowed to spend time alone with a boy. I had signed out for the library but never went there. Where was I, and what was I doing? I had no answer.

The Police suggested that I was "schizoidphrenic," as he called it. He felt that I probably had done these things but couldn't or wouldn't admit them. I kept denying that I had done it, but I had no proof.

Beyond this, they had also entered my room and searched it. There was no indication that I knew French, which was very important as the person who wrote letters had written them in French. However, they kept insisting that I had written them. They did find some of my poetry, which suggested I might be "schizoiphrenic". I consistently denied that I had done it, and as a result, they never pressed charges, and I was allowed to return to the college. I learned two things: the first was that

I did not want to go to college anymore. Although I knew it later, the second was why I should have said yes to Lotus Snow's request; either that or I should have gone with the professor chosen for me. At that time, however, I was being set up but did not understand why.

I went home and told my mother. I thought she would sue them or, at the very least, take legal action. She just looked at me and asked me if I had done it. I turned away from her.

Shortly after I went home, I received a letter from Carlton Allen Ellis's Mother. She told me she knew why I was going to his house and wanted it to stop. I wanted it to stop. I wanted it to stop as well. I wasn't interested in him anyway. He was an interesting case study for my psychology class, and I wrote a fascinating paper on him, but he was not anyone I had any feelings for. I had, as it turned out, no feelings for anyone.

Chapter 8: Memories of the Lower East Side

I went back to college. I had not flunked out because my writing saved me in classes other classes. But I had barely stayed in school. Early during the first year, I received a letter from Dee. She was living in New York and was having a party. Could I come? I got on the bus and went.

She lived with her boyfriend, Ernesto, a tall and substantial black man. He was from somewhere in the Caribbean and was very friendly. Her friend from Sodus Point, Pat, lived with her boyfriend, Bill. There was also a lesbian couple whose name I can't remember. I had brought beer for the party, but no one was drinking it. Instead, they waited for Ernesto to fill his pipe. I said to him, "That is the cutest pipe I have ever seen," Ernesto laughed. "Have some," he said. I told him I did smoke a pipe, and he laughed again. "Just go ahead." I took the tiny pipe in my hand while everyone watched. I took a puff and very quickly exhaled it. 'No," he said, "you have to hold it in." I retook it and held it in. In a matter of minutes, I was high. I had never felt so excellent.

I had developed a "munchies" case, so I left my friends behind and made a large batch of fried potatoes in the kitchen. When I had finished, I came out and saw each one of them making love. I pulled up a seat, ate my potatoes, and watched. There was so much I had to learn.

It was a matter of time before I was spending more and more time in New York. Eventually, I took the step of leaving Keuka College and living there permanently. On the way, I stopped to talk to a woman on the bus. I told her I was moving to New York and leaving college behind. Rather than giving me a lecture, she told me what a wonderful thing I was doing and that I had a great sense of adventure. It gave me the courage to move on.

The neighborhood in New York where I came to live was called the East Village, as opposed to the more fashionable West Village, where artists, writers, playwrights, and musicians once lived because of cheap housing. The West Village was considered America's "bohemian capital" from around the turn of the century until the mid-1960s. Since then, it has become far too expensive for the average person. The West Village was separated from the East Village by New York University and Cooper Union, and the dividing line between the two was somewhere back and forth between Second and Third Avenues. Today, the East Village is sometimes referred to as The Lower East Side and includes Chinatown and Little Italy, but it was not my version of the East Village. The East Village ran from the East River at fourteen Street to Second Avenue; turning left on Second Avenue, it ran down Houston Street and a little beyond that and then back again to the East River. It was primarily "Alphabet City," Avenues A through D, and some streets ran in and through it.

The Lower East Side was where I lived for nearly 13 years of my life; it was where I grew up, married my husbands, and had my children. Aside from going to college at the Old Westbury and New York University and a few vacations, it was a place I was happy to be and never wanted to leave. It was the area I went to after I got off the bus at Port Authority.

It was a transition period for the East Village and, of course, for me. When I first arrived, it was primarily made up of Jewish immigrants. There were Jewish bakeries that sold challah and pastries; a famous bialy store on 14th Street sold only bialys, and the owner stood at the counter covered with flour. Some stores made a variety of pickles, everything from dills to half sours and full sours, that they sold from large wooden barrels. They sold kitchenware from the push carts as well. When I first came to New York, I bought two enameled frying pans from a pushcart on Avenue C. At the age of 78, I still have one to fry eggs in.

The Jews had ties to the garment industry and often worked from their apartments. There were a lot of shops located on Orchard Street where dresses, scarves, trousers and shirts, coats and suits, and children's clothing were available at bargain rates. Everywhere one looked, from the beginning of Avenue C to Houston Street and beyond, people were buying and selling. All along the old tenement apartments were clothes airing and drying, people screaming at one another, and children playing in the midst of it all. From their tiny apartments, people took a break from their work and gazed at the show below. It is one of the most exotic places I have ever lived outside the country.

The pushcarts were still there when I came in 1965, but only briefly. The old Jewish immigrants were still there, but they were old; there were no younger Jews to take their places among the pushcarts, for they had moved on to other homes and other professions. I had lived in parts of the country where no Jews were allowed. A coal miner was hired to work in the mines. Somehow, the men noticed that he did not have a foreskin and refused to work with him, and as a result, he was laid off. On the Jersey Shore, no Jews were allowed to own or rent any property there, as this was a Christian community. But in the East Village, I discovered Jews and a little bit of Jewishness in a world that was decidedly old and European.

I remember first going to a Jewish Deli called Katz's. It was famous then and is famous now. I walked in and ordered a roast beef on rye with butter. I was shocked that they didn't give it to me. They didn't offer me a reason, but the explanation was my ignorance, for no Jew would put meat and dairy in the same sandwich. The men at Katz's had numbers on their forearms. I did not know then, but I know now how they got them and what they meant.

In the upper left-hand corner of the East Village was the Ukrainian and Polish section of the city, also primarily composed of immigrants. In the Ukrainian restaurants, I enjoyed borsch, stuffed cabbage, and kielbasa, all reasonably priced. A well-known Polish pierogi place (ravioli without tomato sauce) offered a variety of pierogi: potato,

potato and cabbage, cabbage, cheese, and Polish coleslaw. It was as if I had returned to my grandmother's kitchen.

In time, The Puerto Ricans, very slowly, came on board. At first, one store, and then another store, and over about five years, it was they and not the Jews who dominated everything. Where the East Village had been filled with the sounds of people calling to one another amongst the pushcarts, The East Village was now filled with the sound of Latin music. It came everywhere: from windows, bodegas, and people hanging in the Street. During the summer, conga drums drifted from Tompkins Square Park, permeating the East Village. Now I ate rice and beans, and fried or baked chicken, and of course, pork. Potato and cabbage were replaced with mangoes, pineapple, and papaya. By the early 1970s, the pushcarts were all gone.

The East Village had replaced the West as a cheap place for artists, writers, and musicians to live. The rise of tenement housing could be traced back to an increase in the population of New York from the mid to the late 1800's due to immigration. Tenements were low-rise buildings with multiple and very narrow two or three-room apartments. Very often, there was only one toilet for the entire floor, although this was to change later when apartments required their own plumbing. Because they were so cheap and food was so inexpensive, they soon began to attract not just immigrants but artists, writers, and musicians from the community.

There were plenty of places to go to hear music, dance, and talk: beat poets, artists, writers, and playwrights moved in, and the Jazz Musicians, yes, they came. Politics played an essential role in the community. At the turn of the century and many years after, the East Village was a home for anarchists, socialists, and communists. Now, there were new revolutionaries as well as the old, such as the Black Panthers, Young Lords, civil rights workers, and Students for a Democratic Society. In the East Village, we all marched into the seventies together.

I lived in a second-floor walk-up on East 3rd Street between Avenues B and C. Typical of tenement buildings, it was made up of two rooms. The first was a rather large room with two huge windows overlooking the Street, and the second was a combination kitchen and bathroom. There was a stove, which was reasonably modern, and next to that, a tub. The tub served as an area for preparing food when its metal cover was intact and as a place for washing dishes, doing laundry, or taking a bath when its metal top was removed. There was a little, single washbasin next to it. A vast cabinet from floor to ceiling covered one-half of the kitchen wall, where one kept kitchen items, dishes, and sewing equipment back in the day. There were no closets, so clothing also had to be held there. In the far corner of the kitchen was the toilet. As for me, who grew up in my grandmother's house with its old coal stove giving off very little heat, it was warm and cozy. I slept on a small mattress between the cabinet and the toilet. I have never been concerned with my material environment and am not now. As long as I had a place to sleep, nothing else mattered.

It took me a long time to figure out that the odors I smelled when I entered the building resulted from rats that had died there. The floors, which were never washed, bore the signs of urine. One had to be careful not to step in it as one walked by. Often, a person was sleeping on one of the floors as there were no locks on the outer door. But I was in New York, and the thrill was terrific.

The very first thing I did was to get a job. I didn't have to go far. A few buildings down from me was a place called The Shrimp Joint. It was like going into a Caribbean restaurant; the leaves of tropical plants were everywhere. It was a fire hazard, but no one noticed or cared. There were four or five booths, but most of our business was take-out. The front was made up of the outside kitchen area; nothing was hidden aside from the rancid oil and potatoes tucked into a room in the back. We cut the potatoes into French Fries using an old potato cutter and poured the rancid oil into the fryers. We sold joints made from the smallest part of the wing, joints made from the large part of the wings, and tons of rancid French Fries. We sold these with powdered Louisiana Hot Sauce. That was it, and our clientele was enormous. Every day, we served dozens and dozens of customers, almost all of them black. I didn't realize it, but this was a sure sign that as the Jews were moving out, blacks and Puerto Ricans were moving in.

Later, I went to a temporary agency to get a better job. I had studied typing in High School since it was one of the more acceptable professions for a woman. I typed almost 90 words a minute, so I found work quickly. One of my first jobs was in a "typing pool." I sat with approximately 20 other women and typed all day with only a break for lunch. The manager rarely spoke to us as she spent most of her time cutting her cigarettes in half and then smoking one after the other in a cigarette holder. This task seemed to occupy her more than watching us—those days when you could smoke on the job and almost anywhere else. I acquired the habit from a woman older than me when I was fourteen years old, and I was addicted.

I worked on and off for a while at a temporary agency but working no longer captured my attention. I had begun to smoke marijuana daily, and I found the joy it brought to me far outweighed anything else. I would get up too late and call in sick. I spent the day smoking and laughing with Ernesto.

I hung out with Ernesto, and we went to the West Village, where he tried to sell pot to tourists. They wanted to buy some marijuana, and Ernesto and I had spent the evening mixing cigarettes with a small amount of marijuana, which we sold to them. In turn, we bought the real stuff to smoke. We sat around watching the people go by, mellow, laughing.

In time, Dee was a little fed up with Ernesto not pulling his weight, and he got a job as a bouncer at a club called Slug's, right next door to where we lived. He looked like a bouncer but was so happy to play the part. When he worked there, he let me in, and I listened to the most excellent jazz musicians in the city: Thelonious Monk, Charlie Mingus, Ornette Coleman, and Sun Ra.

I would meet Ernest years later when he was walking down the Street on the East Side and stopped to say hello. I thought back to when he handed me the pipe and I got stoned, and I smiled.

I, in turn, took my place as an artist in the community. I shared an apartment with several artists who did not live on the Lower East Side but kept a place there to work; the rent was cheap enough. I was now taking classes at the Art Students League. In time, I began showing my work at the Old Reliable, which was turning into a museum. Ah, the Old Reliable.

It was also right across the Street from me. It was an old Polish Jewish bar that had transformed into a place where everyone who was anyone came to the party. The front of the bar was completely gay. No one was wearing drag as in the West Village, which had a reputation for this, but it was gay. But in the back, it was straight. Couples danced, clung to one another, made out passionately, and fought furiously. People came from all over the city to dance and carry on. And the dancing was terrific. A man named Harold could move all his limbs in different directions; Joe could move as if he weren't moving, just slipping across the floor. I, who had never danced, soon became enamored of it. I went there every night and stayed until closing, dancing, and dancing. I got up at seven or so and went to work. I came home, slept until eleven, crossed to the Old Reliable, laughed, and danced the night away. Eventually, I began to work less and less as I spent my time there.

Chapter 9: The Men in My Life-Corey

There were four men in my life, two of whom I married. The first one taught me how to make love to a man, the second taught me how a man should make love to me, the third was the man I chose to have children by, and the fourth was one I dreamed of the kind of life I wanted for myself but who sorely disappointed me. All the men in my life served one purpose: making me feel superior to them. I certainly did not love any of them. They were slaves to my needs, whatever those needs might be to be my lovers, to give me children, to buy me what I wanted when I wanted it, and then, when I was finished with them, have them go away and leave me alone. After all, it was my destiny to be alone, and that was, in the end, part of my psychopathic personality. We are always alone and prefer it that way.

I would find a man, tell him I loved him no matter what, and then go on to find out horrible things about him that I could never forgive, and then leave him, or as the case might be, have him leave. I degraded them terribly. I would spend hours, for example, downgrading my husband in front of other people. Telling them how much I hated him and his habits. It was a pattern I followed.

The first man I encountered was Corey. One of those days when I did find work and didn't have money to eat, I took myself to the Old Reliable, where boiled eggs were on the table. Then I ordered a beer, which came with an order of French Fries, So I sat there around dinnertime, eating eggs and French fries, and reading "Meetings with Remarkable Men" by Gurdjieff. As I was deep in my reading, I heard a man ask me what I was reading, and I told him Gurdjieff's "Meetings with Remarkable Men," and he laughed and said, "How appropriate." We both laughed, and he asked if he could sit down with me, and I said yes. He was black, almost red, with a slightly balding head. He was neither tall nor short nor fat nor thin. I figured him to be around 25. He was very well dressed. But his personality struck me; he was just the most charming man I had ever met. Of course, charisma goes with a psychopathic personality, which he was. We spent about an hour talking, and he asked me if I wanted to go and meet a friend of his the next day, and of course, I said yes.

I had never thought of myself as having a boyfriend. The thought never occurred to me, at least partially because of my desire to be alone. I had a crush on my much older teacher and a boy my age. But, since the time I was younger, I considered myself to be an unattractive woman. I was not homely in a physical sense, but I was athletic and very unfeminine. For example, I never wore makeup. I never have, and at 78, I never will. So, when Corey began to ask me out to meet his friends, I took him to mean what he said and nothing else.

Our first visit was to meet Marianthe. She could have been more friendly. I noticed that her entire conversation revolved around Henry, her boyfriend. If she wasn't talking about Henry, she had nothing to discuss.

Her apartment was very cool. It had one bed and nothing else. The whole apartment was painted white, including the floor. You moved from the living room to a kitchen with a wooden guard rail and into the bathroom with a toilet and tub. There was nothing in the apartment but a bed and a few shelves that held books and sewing stuff. I was very impressed with this minimalist statement of survival.

She was busy sewing by hand, and she talked incessantly about Henry. "Poor Henry, he always wanted to get the clap (gonorrhea), and now he got it, and it hurt so bad when he peed." I could not believe that we were having this conversation, that she wasn't angry but rather so sympathetic to her Henry's case of the clap, and all this while she was busy trying to sew. I say try because she was doing a terrible job of it. Not that I could sew, I couldn't, but I did know that neither could she.

At that point, Henry appeared, and I recognized him immediately from the Old Reliable. He had been sitting at a table alone, and his beauty struck me. My grandmother always told me that if you are attracted to a man, you sit and wait for him. He will come over and speak to you if he is interested in you. If he weren't interested, he wouldn't. I have followed that advice save in the case of Henry. He had dark curly hair, beautiful eyes, and a handsome mouth; he was tall and had a beautiful build. He was and is among the most attractive men I have ever met. I forgot my grandma's words and went over to speak to him. I talked to him for only a few minutes before I realized that he was an arrogant and obnoxious man whom I didn't want to get to know any better, and I turned away. He was disgusting. Now I found the woman to which he belonged: Marianthe's boyfriend. Henry and Marianthe would remain an integral part of my life forever.

Cory asked me to go with him the following evening to visit Russel Fitzgerald, a painter, and his wife, Dara. The first thing one saw when entering their living room was a massive painting of the American flag draped across a table, and one side of the flag, on a plate, was a white penis and testicles, and on the other, a dish of a black penis and testicles. It was both well done and striking. Some of his paintings looked like flowering vaginas. Set off in the corner was a portrait of Henry leaning out the window, half in the room and half out, completely naked. I complimented Russel on his work; they were both technically perfect and powerful pieces. We spent the rest of the evening enjoying some of Russel's excellent cooking and talking about art. It was lovely.

We went to meet Sara and Chuck the next night. Sarah was a member of the daughters of the American Revolution, and Chuck, who was black, was her lover. Sarah worked as a teacher, and Chuck worked when and if he could. They became our close friends, and we went to see them almost every weekend.

We went on like this long before he hit on me. He became the first man I ever had an orgasm with. He taught me, over time, how to have sex with a man. In the end, we were together for only a few months, but I learned just how dangerous a man can be.

As it turned out, we moved into his apartment, which was not his apartment but that of a criminal who had been sent to prison. However, I didn't know that at the time. It was small but friendly; it had a kitchen, a living room, a bedroom, and that miracle of all miracles, a separate bathroom with a tub and a toilet. I had stepped up in life.

However, it soon dawned on me that Corey didn't work, and neither did I. He had been laid off from his job, he said, and would soon, when we were finished with the honeymoon, look for another, or so I was told. In the meantime, Sarah had a friend looking for a babysitter, and I took the job. It was a full-time job, and so I worked all day. Cory went along for the ride.

It was warm, and the city was beautiful, and we used to take the children to parks and watch them play.

We went to the Old Reliable late at night, danced, and hung out with friends. Then we went home and made love. Life was, in a sense, quite blissful, and I almost forgot that he was not working. I paid for whatever food we ate, but nothing more. He paid for nothing but did, on occasion, bring home some joints. More and more, too, he began to spend time away from the apartment. And in time, I sat at home while he went out to do something. But we had started to argue about him going out and leaving me, his not working, and his general laziness. During one of our arguments, he struck me, and I hit him back, and he struck me twice as hard. When the violence ended, I looked at him and said I was leaving. I would have left him that second, but he responded by watching me ever more closely and continuously with the threat of violence. He was with me if I went to the store; he was close by if I went to Chuck and Sarah's.

We didn't go out to the Old Reliable anymore. Then, one morning, I woke up, and he was asleep. I dressed myself and snuck out the door. I went to Greenwich Village and sat there for most of the day. When it was evening, I returned to Chuck and Sarah's, where he had been looking for me, and then went off to the Old Reliable. Sarah let me stay in one of her rooms, and early in the morning, I borrowed money from her and took the long trip back to New Jersey to my mother's home. I had gone out into the world and come home defeated.

61

Chapter 10: Memories of Hell

My arrival at my mother's was defined by my dreams and not by the reality of my days. The terror of living with Cory haunted me, and I wanted to get back at him for all he had done to me. To hit him and abuse him as he used to do to me. I woke in sweats, my heart pounding with the violence I felt for him. The circumstances of living with my mother also haunted me while I slept.

I dreamt that I was stuck in her house and could not escape. I would run from door to door, window to window, to find them all boarded up. I could not get out. In one recurring dream, I was walking by a garden, and suddenly, giant snakes came out and wrapped themselves around me so that I was caught. I dreamt this over and over again.

I dream of my grandmother and grandfather often. But there is one dream that haunts me until this day, for I never knew whether it was a dream or true. I woke up in the middle of the night to find my grandmother sitting in a rocking chair near my bed. I watched her while she went back and forth, back, and forth. She told me she had come down to see if I was okay. I asked her how she had gotten there, for I lived on an island, and for her to get there, she would have had to call a cab, and there were no taxis. Moreover, it was winter, so everything was closed, and the tourists had gone home. Aside from the few people who lived there all winter, it was a dim and lonely place, and people were few and far between. She said she had gotten a ride here and was staying with me for a while. I felt so happy that she was staying. She asked me if I was okay, and I told her yes even though my life was miserable. And then she asked me to go to sleep, that she would talk to me in the morning. I rolled over and slept. When I awoke, she was gone. I searched the whole house but could not find her. I asked my mother if she had seen her, and she looked at me as if I were crazy. Yet,

I saw my grandmother that night; I am sure of it. For one night, I slept a long, dreamless sleep.

My Mother occupied herself by working and then going to the bars, and I saw very little of her. I don't know where my sister, Barbara, was, to tell you the truth. She had little meant to me as a person.

My Mother never asked about what my life had been like in New York. She had little to say to me except to ask for the rent. I thought this was outrageous considering the amount of money she had taken from me. I was just left, as I always was, to write or paint or go running along the beach. It was winter, and I ran the beach for miles until I could no longer run. It was gray and dismal; very often, fog clung to shore, and I felt so alone as I walked.

In the meantime, I worked at Perkins, took overtime shifts, and, as it turned out, made quite a bit of money when one considered the tips. It only took me over six months to save up enough to return to New York.

When I told my Mother I was going, she didn't even bother to take me to the station, and I had to ask one of my neighbors to do it and pay them.

Chapter 11: Memories of Returning to New York

I had been in touch with Chuck and Sarah, so when I arrived in New York, they had a friend who was giving up his apartment, and he let me live there.

It was horrible: two rooms with a stove that didn't work and a refrigerator. I cooked food with hot water from the sink and ate it. There was one toilet and a tub in the kitchen. It was still winter, and I was frozen because I had seven windows in a ground-floor, two-room apartment, which left me open for robberies. But it cost me thirty-three dollars a month, which was reasonable even then.

Chuck and Sarah also had a friend who ran a kennel a few blocks away, and he was looking for help, someone to help feed the dogs and watch over things. I was ever so glad to find a job waiting for me; I would have done anything not to go back into a typing pool. The job seemed perfect as I could go in later in the afternoon and still go to the Old Reliable. As it turned out, Buzzy was a very light-skinned black man from the Southern part of the U.S. He seemed to come from money and was always immaculately dressed. When he spoke, it was with a perfect English accent, not any of the Ebonics used by the black community. He seemed very well-educated. Moreover, he had quite a successful business. He trained dogs for the security purposes of individuals, and he was more than willing, in fact very eager, to pass on what he knew about training dogs to me. I would feed the dogs and wait for him to train them. He would show me the tricks of the trade. Aside from talking about the dogs, he never had much to say to me. It was all business. He taught me to train them how to behave: how to heel and sit, how to turn along with its owner. Some he prepared to attack. With my psychopathology, I loved handling the dogs making them do what I wanted. There was no genuine affection between me and the animals I trained. It was all a matter of control.

On one particular occasion, he called in another dog trainer to assist him with training the dogs. Buzzy told me this man had trained dogs for the Nazis, although he was a Jew. He survived because he was a modern-day "dog whisperer." He was already old, although I can't guess how old, short, and wizen. He would sit and look into the dog's eyes, and then, after some time, he could describe how the dog should be trained. It was remarkable. When Buzzy left the room to get one of the dogs, he walked over to me and, looking me straight in the eye, he said, "Please allow me," and I let him feel my breasts. I couldn't believe I just sat there and let him do that. From that moment onward, I never held my tongue. If someone did something insulting to me, I was always quick to answer him. But at that moment I, too, felt like one of the dogs he was training.

One animal came in, a beautiful white shepherd about seven months old. Buzzy had been asked to sell the dog because the owner's child had allergies. She was lovely, pure white, with a pink nose, and I negotiated terms with Buzzy and bought her, for she was pretty expensive. I brought her home to my two-room apartment, and she guarded the place for me when I wasn't there. Her very presence kept my apartment safe. On one occasion, I brought her into the apartment, and she lunged forward; I looked up to see two men there waiting for me. They ran out at the sight of the dog, but there was no question that they were waiting for me.

When she came into heat, I asked Buzzy if he had a male German Shepard to mate with Kim, and he found me a champion with aristocratic royal bloodlines. Kim came from a good lineage even though she was white, which was considered unacceptable for a Shepard. After she came into heat, I mated her with the male, and she gave birth to eleven puppies, most of them as white as she was. I sold the puppies and got enough money to move out of my apartment and into a decent place, one East 2nd St. It had a long entry foyer, a living room set off from the kitchen, and a bedroom. On top of it all, it had a bathroom large enough to dance in with a tub, shower, and toilet. I had moved up in life.

After I had worked for Canine East, Buzzy decided he was opening a new kennel on the upper west side, one that handled puppies for sale, and I was sent uptown to take care of that place. I was embarking on my career as a dog handler and trainer, which seemed acceptable. I still went to the Old Reliable and smoked, although not so much. I still pained and wrote poetry and hung out with artists and writers in the community. I walked around the Lower East Side streets and thought that life was quite good and happy.

Chapter 12: Memories of Little Eddie

I don't know why, I really don't. I smoked marijuana rather than drank at this point in my life, but I was drinking a little that night, and perhaps I got drunk, I don't know. But he was sitting alone, nursing his drink at the table, and I asked him to come home with me. It was the first time I had ever made love to a man. Corey, to be sure, taught me the technical details, but Corey, in truth, was a technician. Little Eddie was plain, raw sexuality, and I loved every minute. He left after that first evening, and I didn't see him for a while. There were no cell phones, and I didn't know where he lived as we came to my place.

I entered the Old Reliable one evening and saw Little Eddie sitting at the bar. One went to the bar to rest from the dancing, or to order a drink, but one did not stay in the gay section of the club because it meant you were gay. I told him that he was sitting at the wrong end of the bar as this was the "gay" section. He looked at me and then looked around and got up immediately. I laughed, saying I didn't think he belonged there considering our evening, and he seemed pleased with the compliment.

We sat in the back and talked and danced for a while. Little Eddie had come just recently from St Lucia. Having served in the army, he came to America and began working in a local hospital called Beth Israel. Eddie was good-looking but earned his name "Little Eddie" because he was very short and thin. Of course, my grandfather was short and thin, so he fit in perfectly with my image of what a male should be like. While he was short and thin, one area of his anatomy was so remarkable I couldn't forget it. I remember the pleasure he had given me; I recalled it repeatedly as I dreamed about him in my fantasies. He was a fantastic lover.

We were all dancing to "Boog aloo" at that time. It involved moving your head furiously back and forth while you moved your body from side to side. While most of America was listening to the Beetles, we at the Old Reliable heard "Sugar Pie Honey Bunch," "My Girl," "Dancing in the Street" by by The Vandellas, "The Tracks of My Tears" by Smokey Robinson, great songs by the Temptation and the Supremes. There was the white world of the boy bands from England and the music coming from America's heartland, Detroit, and the division between them was marked by race.

As we danced, we became more sexually drawn to each other, and in time, we went home to my place, now on East 3rd Street, and made love until the sun came up. It used to be the case that I would wake up in the middle of the night, and we would be making love, not fully awake, and we would have an orgasm and go back to sleep. If we were arguing, and we happened to touch one another's arms, we would make love on the floor; so deep was my passion for this man. We would forget what we were arguing about in the frenzy of desire.

But no matter what my sexual feelings were for him, I had no deeper emotions regarding love or marriage. I didn't love him, and I never pretended I did. He told me he had told his family about me and asked me to come and meet them, but I had no desire to go there. That was his world; mine was the Old Reliable and the artists, writers, and musicians who gathered there.

He was already someone I used to mock and make fun of. Seeped in his Catholicism, he dreamed of having a daughter and dressing her up to attend Church with him. I would argue that if we had a daughter, he would dress all up and take her to the Catholic Church; I would take her and run so far, he could not find me. Anyway, he wouldn't have a daughter or son with me. I promised him that. I could see how disappointed I made him, and I didn't care. I made fun of his stupidity. I ridiculed him for not wanting anything else and having no literary or artistic ability. There was no end to my mockery of him, and it grew worse and worse until all I did was mock him and make love to him. There was nothing in between.

Even my love for Corey was "fake," so to speak. I had no real feelings for him aside from the fact that he was very charming. As for Eddie, I grew to dislike him more and more over time. He loved to get paid and take me out to dinner; then, he would get himself a bottle, watch TV, and stay home. He bored me aside from when we made love. I wanted him to make love to me and then return to his apartment and pick up his life. At first, he kept his apartment; I had mine, and everything was fine. But his apartment was way too expensive for the Lower East Side. It was still a studio apartment, a modern building with elevators and a locked door. The living, dining, and kitchen rooms were all in one space.

But over time, he began to spend more and more time at my place and less on his own. Eventually, he came to me and said he could no longer afford his place. No question, I agreed; he couldn't afford his home on the small income he was getting at Beth Israel, but I didn't want him to move in with me. I tried to get him an apartment in one of the tenement buildings, but he refused. We had huge fights about this, and he did move in because there was no choice.

But our relationship declined from wild lovemaking to one in which he, like Corey, tried to hold me in check. Eventually, he learned how much my grandmother and aunts meant to me, and he threatened to call them up and tell them I took drugs. I only smoked marijuana and never bothered with anything else, nor did I drink, but I knew that the very hint of me smoking pot would send them over the edge. I didn't know what to do about him.

There was another reason I held on to Eddie, and this was the fact that he appeared as my "boyfriend." Cory had disappeared when he had gone to jail. But after he got out, he found himself a new woman and introduced her to the Old Reliable. Her name was Marilyn; some fifty-five years later, she remains one of my friends. But he didn't come near me as long as I was with little Eddie.

In time, he began to deal drugs. He would buy some pot and then sell it for a little more than he bought it for and make a profit. He did that repeatedly, and he soon made a good money. In time, he began to go out more and more to sell, and I was content to sit home and paint, or if I was bored, go down to the Old Reliable and hang out for a while. I never cheated on him, and I never felt the need. He was, without question, the best lover I ever had, and I would wait for him to come home and make love to me.

But one day, he didn't come home. I thought, perhaps, he had gotten involved with a woman. But he didn't come home that evening, the next, or the next. He left his clothes at my house, and I was sure he had gotten into trouble. I called the police and found out nothing. Sometime during the second week, they fished him out of the East River. I heard this from one of my friends. He had gotten involved with someone who thought instead of buying some pot; they could go ahead and take it all and dump him into the river. He was shipped back to St. Lucia for the funeral.

Chapter 13: Memories of Jose Antonio Roman, Jr.

I worked a few hours daily helping a gas station owner on the corner of East 2nd and Avenue B, close out his register. I was busy counting money when he came in and ignored him until I was done. Then I picked up my head and looked at him: I had met the father of my children. He was beautiful and well-dressed, and everything about him was immaculate. However, one crucial question had to be answered: did he work and earn enough money to survive? I would have left him if, like Corey, if he didn't work or, like Little Eddie, worked but did not earn enough to survive.

Are you looking for work?" I said, thinking that he was looking for a job pumping gas. "No." he said, "I have a construction company. I am looking for the owner to talk to him about doing some work." That was the deciding factor, as now he became all the more desirable to me. In turn, he looked at me, and without the strangeness of it appearing to him, he asked me if I had a shower. "Yes", I answered. "Can I come up to your place and take a shower." I needed clarification on whether this was a come-on or if he did need to bathe. And here he was, hardly knowing me, and asking me if he could come and wash at my place. I should have been dissuaded from having any interest in him, but I wasn't. I said, yes, I had a shower, and he could come and take a bath. I trusted him absolutely, this man who was going to abandon me.

I closed out, Jose spoke to the owner, and I took him to my apartment right up the block. He quietly went in, showered, and then returned to talk to me. He talked about construction, and I talked about my life as an artist and the Old Reliable. "Oh, I never go out. I work and then sleep." He was working at that time for George A. Fuller, the giants of construction as they were called, and told me about some of the jobs he had been on. There was a picture of him in the New

York Times, where he was doing some work there. And all the while, I thought how perfect this man would be to marry and have children. He left, and I did not ask him to stay. But he came around Alfredo's to do some work in the evenings, and over time and with many bathes in between, we became lovers. To put it bluntly, he was one of the worst lovers I ever had. I NEVER enjoyed our lovemaking. But this didn't dissuade me; he moved in with me in time.

When we went to move from his place to mine, I found him living in the basement of a tenement. I was shocked because he made so much money and could easily afford his home. Moreover, it was why he was looking for a tub to take a bath in; he had no tub of his own or, for that matter, running water. Only a bunch of clothing was hanging from one of the pipes and a bed in the corner where he slept. A huge piano dominated the room. "Do you play?" I asked, "No, he said, but he found it on the street and took it. The only other thing was a table and chair; he worked whenever he could to design something to build. He was an excellent designer, and I remember being quite impressed with his work. He was a very talented man, and it seemed to me, at the time, that the way he lived reminded me of an Ayn Rand novel: this character who lived only for his work and didn't care about his environment. He dreamed of becoming an architect or a designer. It was all he cared about, which would be the testimony of his life, that he lived to work and worked to live, and nothing else mattered to him.

In turn, I looked at him and saw what a mess my life was. I was an artist, but not one who was particularly dedicated. I spent my life hanging out with friends at the Old Reliable, dancing, and then going home, unsure if I would get up for work. I had lost the job at Buzzy's due to my lack of focus and concentration, and I spent my time in temporary agencies where I made just enough to live. I knew this had to stop, and with Jose as the impetus, I changed my lifestyle.

I stopped going to the Old Reliable. It was challenging, mainly as my whole life revolved around it. Still, I had Jose sitting at home designing things, and I wanted to go home and feed us and then listen to his dreams. They were, of course, his dreams. Nothing about my dreams seemed to matter. I was an artist, and that was that. I would marry this man and have his babies, and he would be the one who followed his dreams. My dreams and ambitions remained hidden. I was twenty years old.

I found myself a real job working for the Department of Social Services at Bellevue Hospital, where I worked as a medical transcriptionist. I used a Dictaphone, which had little plastic strips with the Doctor's voices inscribed on it. I would place them on the Dictaphone and record what the doctors said, relying on a foot pedal to stop to start the machine. It was interesting, and I didn't have to sit in a typing pool and type.

My "boss" was a black man who also was deeply involved in his church. He was a nice guy, as I remember it, but he felt preyed up to give me lessons from the Bible, which was a massive waste of time for me. But he came to work every day and tried. I got so aggravated with him that I wrote him a letter explaining the folly of his beliefs. It was quite a long letter, but by no means a harmful or insulting letter. He approached me the next day and said he would become a writer if he could, as I did. I felt guilty because I was not a writer. I wrote a bit of poetry, but my focus was on art, and I felt ashamed that I had not bothered with my writing for a long time.

Chapter 14: Memories of Tiel

Back in the day, we didn't have an instant test to find out if we were pregnant, but instead had to go for a "rabbit test." The test took a few days, and when I found out, I ran home to celebrate. I decorated the apartment with balloons, cooked dinner, and waited for him to return. He did seem as happy as I was.

During this time, he was doing construction for a lawyer who took a liking to him. The lawyer was in charge of this tiny, three-storied building on the same side as the Old Reliable. If we took care of the building, we could rent this huge, five-room apartment for a reasonable rent. We jumped at the offer.

Jose set out to turn the house into a showpiece of design. Almost all the furniture was handmade and hung off the walls. In the kitchen, which he did next, he found a beautiful butcher block table and hung it off the wall. Then he built around it a series of shelves, each made to fit a particular kitchen item: a spot for a toaster, an area for my blender, my food grinder, and everything; he made a place just for it. A series of shelves held my glasses and another for each dish I used according to its function, and a set for bowls.

But the bedroom was his most outstanding part. First, he took the interior down to the beams and joists, leaving the bare brick. When the beams and joists throughout the room were exposed, he applied stucco. The beams were revealed, but the stucco was in between. He left small areas for candles. Then he began with the bed. It was an eight-foot by eight-foot octagonal, and it was hung from the beamed ceiling by aeronautical wires. He made these very taunt so that they did not move. When he put candles into the niches he built for them, it was as if the bed was hanging in space.

As a gift for me for Christmas, he made me an easel. I moved it in the most minute detail, exactly how I wanted it. I continued to paint, and Jose continued to revel in my creations and bring forth new designs of his own. "People will say of us that we were artists living here, and they will admire us for what we created," he said. I was sitting there watching him complete the bed when I felt the baby move for the first time, and I thought that if it were a girl or a boy, this baby would be a great artist. What else could it be?

Just before the baby was born, there was a change between us. Partially, it resulted from the fact that he never really finished anything. There was always some incomplete action that, if he finished it, would have left his projects complete, but he never finished them. The kitchen was done, but the bedroom was still unfinished. I came home one day to find my home turned into a construction site, two-by-fours, and a huge chainsaw sitting in the living room. He had used the saw to build something, and it covered everything from the dishes in the kitchen to the bedroom to the furniture in the living room with dust. "What are you doing," I asked. And he didn't even bother to respond to me. Dust covered everything; it was my job to clean or forget about it.

He wouldn't do it because cleaning the house was my responsibility, and if I didn't, it would not get done. We had a huge fight, and he walked out, and I looked at the dust around me. I had a baby in just over a month, and I couldn't imagine the Herculean task of cleaning up his mess only to know that Jose would make more of it.

He went out and didn't come back for almost another day. I was so worried that I could not function. When Jose called me later that evening, he said he had bought some clothes and a bus ticket, only to decide he couldn't leave me. I told him to come home, and we made up. But the fact was, our beautiful apartment was still a construction site, and he was beginning his first journey into the hell of his schizophrenia. But I didn't know this. I kept urging him to clean up the place before the baby was born, and he continued with his sawing and construction as if I were not talking to him.

I went into labor almost a month late, begging him to clean up the place before the baby came home. We had decided if I had a boy, we would name him Jose the III, and if I had a girl, I would name her Marianthe after my friend, who had a son who was a little over one year old. The contractions came more frequently, and I kept waiting for them to get nasty to go to the hospital. I looked at my husband, who had sat through many births from his brothers and sisters and found him crying. "Please, please go to the hospital." And I went.

We couldn't find a cab to take us since the cab driver saw me in the throes of pregnancy and took off. But we finally got one, and I got to the hospital just as my daughter was born. It was a small hospital used for drying out very wealthy alcoholics. But they did have a minor maternity ward, and that is where I went. My doctor had not arrived yet, and there I was with my nurse, who wanted me to wait. When she examined me for the last time, she said that I was due and gave me a shot to put me out while we waited for the doctor. I slept and woke up in the morning to find out I had a daughter.

"What will you name her?" the nurse asked me. I did not say Marianthe but chose teal because I felt like I had awakened from a forest of teal-colored trees. How do you spell that, the nurse asked? I was still suffering from the effects of being put to sleep, so I didn't know how to spell Teal, and I thought, "I before E except after C. And so, the name Tiel was written down for my baby. Her middle name was Christine. Tiel Christine, I thought to myself: how beautiful.

When Jose came to the hospital with flowers that said to Mary and Marianthe, I was afraid to tell him I had changed her name, but I did. "What did you call her," he asked. "Tiel," I said. And he thought that it was the most beautiful name he had ever heard. Tiel Christine Roman, he said repeatedly, and we smiled. "It sounds like the name of an artist," I said.

Finally, I got to see my baby. Some politicians were fond of saying, "Every woman has the most beautiful baby, and that is hers." But there is no question that Tiel was beautiful. She was stunning, with a long pointy chin, deep cheeks, and a perfect head. I looked at her and could not speak for the beauty of her. I was watching her silently, and she, in turn, was watching me. After she returned to the nursery, I found myself crying. I felt that the world did not deserve her. I wondered how the poor child would survive in such a horrid world.

I took Tiel home in a cab, and Jose followed with his truck. When I walked into the apartment, I found it as I left it: a vast construction site filled with dust. By the time he came upstairs, I was finished with him. After I put the baby down in her crib, I screamed and yelled at him, and he left.

I cleaned the apartment as best I could and made a place for the baby and myself in the back bedroom. I only spoke to Jose briefly. Slowly, I made my way through the pile of dust and restored the apartment to how it looked before. I put all his tools away in the spare room, and he never touched them.

Chapter 15: Memories of Staten Island

Chuck and Sarah remained my friends when I became involved with Jose, and we used to go over to their house for dinner or drink at different bars. They had recently bought a house in Staten Island, New York, and we went over there quite frequently so that Jose could help Chuck with the house. Jose had a truck that we called "Esmeralda" because it was green. I used to sing to Tiel as we drove there:

"Jiggle, jiggle, Esmeralda, when little Tiel was a Baby,

Jiggle, jiggle, Esmeralda, to Staten Island, we would go.

Jiggle, jiggle, Esmeralda, and little Tiel has a lion's bib

Jiggle, jiggle, Esmeralda, and little Tiel has a blue crib.

Jiggle, jiggle, Esmeralda to Staten Island, we would go."

During this period, however, I was still angry with Jose. I no longer had any respect for the architect who dreamed dreams; instead, I fell prey to the old habit of mocking and ridiculing him for all the things he started to do but never finished. He was no longer the man I admired and wanted to be like. I saw him for what he was: a man who wished praise for what he had done, and when Jose did enough work to garner it, he moved on to the next thing. Aside from the kitchen, he never finished anything. I ridiculed my Ayn Rand hero, who did not complete a project, and I never stopped.

Sarah used to tell me that I held the Baby too much, and I smiled because I was obsessed with her and didn't want to let go. Sometimes, Jose would go to work and come and say goodbye, and I was sitting there looking at the baby in my arms, and when he came home, I was sitting there holding her as well. Although I did not speak to her as many parents do today, my mode of dealing with her was silent.

Somehow, Chuck and Sarah convinced us to move out to Staten Island with them. There was an apartment next door to Chuck and Sarah in a two-family home, so we left our beautiful apartment, which was only partially done, and moved to Staten Island to live. At least in Staten Island, we could start anew.

The house had a lot of potential, and it was old, which is what I like. It had a vast and elaborate fireplace in the living room, a kitchen, and two rather large living rooms. The fireplace was the star of the show, with old Dutch tiles and an oversized front. It took up the whole room. One Saturday morning, I came home from shopping to find that Jose had removed the tiles from the front of the fireplace. "Why, why did you do this." "They were uneven," he said. We had a huge fight. He was repeating the same thing all over again. Nothing was finished; everything was incomplete.

I walked around, trying my best to keep it all together, but this time, I had Chuck and Sarah, which made it all bearable. I would complain to Sarah about how Jose never finished things, and I complained to Chuck when he was around. Moreover, I got pregnant again and had a miscarriage. I was in the hospital for quite a while before I came home, and the Baby stayed at Sarah's while I got myself together. A few weeks after I came home, I had to go to the doctors for a check-up and left Tiel with her father. It was the first time I had ever asked him to watch the Baby, as I always held on to it. When I returned several hours later, I found him in the living room and Tiel crying in her crib. I discovered that he had not changed her or given her some formula for quite some while. He sat there and waited for me to get home to take care of everything. We had a huge fight over this, and I asked him how he could not take of her when I was gone. He didn't respond. By now, he was gone into his world, often sitting somewhere all alone for hours and hours at a time. He hardly ever spoke to me about what he was thinking.

Jose soon began taking classes at the local university. It was during this time that he found another lover. One night, he did not come home at all. That is how I finally found out. My Aunt Eva went over a little after midnight and stayed until he came in, when she just disappeared. I still need to find out how she managed to get from Jersey City to Staten Island alone, but she did

He listened to my rantings but didn't say one word. A few days later, my mind was made up. I would get a job and find a way out of this situation. There I was, stuck in Staten Island and missing New York. Living in a construction site was one thing, terrible though it was his having a lover was another. As it turned out, I had a dream one evening that he had made a baby with this woman. It turned out to be accurate; he had gotten involved with a much younger woman and gotten her pregnant. But it would be a long time before I found out; at which point it didn't matter.

It took a while, but I managed to get out with the help of my best friend Marilyn, who lent me the money and helped me to get an apartment on the Lower East Side, and I moved "back home." In the meantime, I was fixing up the apartment with my friend Marianthe when I turned to her and said, I haven't gotten my period. "Oh, you are probably just stressed; it will come." It didn't. I discovered I was pregnant and couldn't figure out how it happened because I never remembered sleeping with Jose. I would have another baby with a husband I couldn't trust.

Chapter 16: Memories of The State University of New York at Old Westbury

For a long time, I kept dreaming of a secret room hidden where I lived, which I discovered. I kept dreaming about this over and over again. It was a harbinger of things to come.

I was just a few weeks pregnant when my friend, Marilyn told me about a waitress job in the village. I could get some money because, by now, I was living off Welfare, and after I paid my rent and bought food, I had nothing left; I could manage to buy a crib and things for the baby. But to do this, I had to find a daycare center.

Marilyn got involved with a daycare center, a parent's cooperative on East 6th Street called Children's Welcome. Initially, it was just a cooperative nursery where each parent volunteered their time, and someone watched their children. The people who did this were anarchists. Being an anarchist teacher meant that no matter what the children wanted, they got it. They did what they, and not the teachers, wanted to do. In the beginning, the children were into playing with poo, and they did so until they got tired of it. Then, they turned to dressing in clothing that was not their gender. Kevin, Marilyn's son, used to choose to dress up in a girl's bathing suit. He is very straight now, married for a long time to the same woman, so it did not seem to influence them very much. Then, they went through a period in which sexual precociousness was dominant. The children used to practice kissing, although I don't think they understood much about anything else. They painted if they wanted to paint and sometimes pained the floor and ceilings of the daycare center. We had one boy who came in and masturbated all day long. He thought by doing this, he would shock the children, but neither the children nor Sherry or Ernie paid any attention to him, so he stopped and got on with his life.

All the while, Sherry and her boyfriend, Ernie, did nothing but sit and smile at these children as if what they did was beautiful and liberating. Although I did want to put Tiel in there, at least because it was so liberating, there were no slots available then, so I began searching for another daycare center. I remember this day because it opened a new phase of my life.

I wandered into a place called The Educational Assistance Center. I can recall the first woman I saw, Doris Deiter. I walked in and asked her if she had any daycare available. "No, she said, we don't offer daycare. We serve adults who want to go to college." I got up and started to walk out; I was looking for a daycare center. Wait, "Don't you want to go to school?" "Oh, I can't go to school. I have a child to support and another on the way. I need daycare so I can work for a while." "Uh-huh," she said, "well, the college we would send you to has a daycare program." I sat down.

"But I am living on Welfare. I won't be allowed to go to college." "We can work that out," she replied. "They will make arrangements." "But how will I pay tuition?" "They will pay it for you." It was too good to be to be believed. As she explained, if I were accepted, I would still get my welfare payments, a grant, and a scholarship." "In addition, I could bring my daughter to daycare. What the hell, I said to myself, and filled out the application. A week later, I was formally admitted to the State University of New York, the College at Old Westbury. In addition to my welfare payments, I received a sum I can't recall, but it was at least as significant as my Welfare payments. I got the check a few months later. I decided that I would buy a crib and things for my baby, and then, because my dental work was so bad, I would go into the hospital and have the dentist do oral surgery on me while under anesthesia. Brooke was due in late November, so I decided to go until she was born and then get lost. Yeah, that's what I thought.

What I discovered was a whole new way of life. In the fall of 1971, I began at Old Westbury. On top of the fact that they were giving me financial assistance, they also tabulated the amount of college I had done at Keuka Park and gave me credit for my experiences with art and other "life achievements." I could graduate in less than two years. Fantastic, except I didn't want to go to begin with. But I went.

I was large then, as this was in September, and I was due in early November. At first, nearly everyone stared at me. Well, I thought, there aren't very many pregnant women around. But then professors asked me. "Your name is Mary Roman." "Yes, I said, as Roman was my married name." "You don't look Puerto Rican." "Oh, I am not." And with that I understood that I accepted and got such a large stipend because they thought I was Puerto Rican.

Old Westbury was part of the Johnson Poverty Program and set out to help people experiencing poverty improve their lives. It was an equal opportunity improvement program. There were, as yet, no Community Colleges, and this was an experiment to see what would happen if the poor were allowed to go to college just like the rich. But much more than that, it was to find out what would happen if this college were filled with radicals, or so it seemed to me. It was as if some Marxist/Anarchist, like Sherry and Erinie, had set up this school and left the students to their own freedom of expression. We didn't have grades, just a pass-or-fail system.

I studied with Donald Bluestone. In the Social History of Guilt, I learned the effects of racism and discrimination in science and education. Donald would later write of me in a letter of recommendation for one of the universities, that I had an "uncanny ability to master the material and, what is even more rare, to synthesize the material and make it her own." He would add that I was one of the most articulate members of the class. "She had the rare quality of independence of mind that is both refreshing and inspiring. Never intimidated by the pressures of the conformity or the teacher, Mary has an intellectual integrity and courage that is hard to find in academia." For the first time, I had a glimpse of who I was. Later on, I would conjecture how my intellectual integrity led me to a passion for truth, which, as it turned out, was a bad as well as a good thing. It led me to tell the truth about what I saw and to engage in what I called Critical Thinking, but it also led me to say things to people that I should not have said to them or should have said differently if I had been a kinder and more considerate person. It was the mark of my psychopathy. But at this point in time, I was pretty proud of what he said about me.

We had revolutionaries from Latin America to teach us how to make a revolution. We had radical union leaders come to tell us about how workers and unions had struggled for their rights, and I remembered how my grandfather had joined the United Mine Workers and what a difference it had made for him. We read books like "Labor's Untold Story," which told how capitalists benefited from the Government and everything else, and "The People's History of the United States" by Howard Zinn. I realized that I had been lied to all my life, that America wasn't the land of opportunity but the land of exploitation, and that if anyone were to get ahead, they had to join the petite bourgeoise and leave the working class behind. We studied things like The Sociology of Women with Barbara Ehrenreich and Deidra English. After a very short period, I found myself to be a Marxists Feminist, something I have been all of my life. I never once took my eye off the prize, a revolution in my time, and I began living my life as a dedicated revolutionary. Or at least that is how I imagined myself. In reality, I was a self-centered woman who cared nothing about the workers or the oppressed people of the earth but only about myself and getting ahead. This feeling of unity and solidarity did not affect my functioning as a psychopath. I dreamed a dream of making a revolution, but I was still waging the war of all against all. I thought of being a great leader of the people and hungered for glory at all costs. If anyone got in the way of my fantasies of glory, I sought to eradicate them: this applied to my fellow students, the "people" I worked for, and anyone who would dare to challenge me.

Old Westbury was an experiment to see what would happen if you took the most oppressed and downtrodden people and educated them—and educated them. I can tell you that this easy money was an opportunity for most people to get drugs and alcohol and not much else. Many individuals died of drug overdoses. For others, this was the opportunity to make something of themselves. A woman had more children than the Old Woman who lived in the Shoe, graduated from Old Westbury, along with me, and had her children with her when she received her diploma. There was another woman who was a prostitute, who graduated and then went on to a career as a lawyer. Many of these people went on to the labor movement. And some of them, like me, went on to graduate school. These things happen when you turn the poor and oppressed into educated people with a sense of Marxist consciousness.

When taking my Doctoral Comprehensives, they asked me how I got into New York University, and I replied without hesitation that I got there because of Lyndon Johnson's poverty program. If it had not been for that, the Educational Assistance Center and Doris Dieter, and the radical professors who gave me an insight into the true nature of life in America, I wouldn't have been there.

Chapter 17: Memories of Me on My Own

Brooke was born on November 20th, 1971, over Thanksgiving Break. I was home for Thanksgiving and asked my Aunt Eva to bring Tiel home. She was not too delighted to let her go, but she did bring her. I cooked a chicken and ate dinner with the baby on the table between Tiel and I. And I celebrated coming home with my new family.

. The support checks were coming few and far between at that time. Jose and I had no legal agreement, so I had no legal foundation for demanding them. I would have had to go to court and had yet to learn where Jose lived or worked. Once, when he stopped by, always without a warning, I nagged him about the checks. He responded that he had started sending them to the bank. I answered that I had no bank account. I looked at him, and he was deadly silent. I knew he wouldn't respond, so I told him to leave.

He stopped by later to tell me how "they" had been persecuting him." When I asked him who "they" were, he didn't have an answer for this either. On another occasion. Jose said to me that he cured himself of brain cancer and what a miracle it was. Finally, Jose told me that he "was God" and had to power to do anything. He was, without question, insane, and I felt the need to get away from him. Any doubts I had had before, were quickly resolved when I found out how crazy he was.

I had a friend, some guy who was also interested in marrying me, and he knew a lawyer who would help me. In a matter of months, I had filed for divorce on grounds of desertion. I had to wait for him to visit and have Marilyn give him the papers. When he came at last, I went down the hall and called Marilyn, and she came up and served him. The only thing Jose said was that there was a typing error in the report and left. He came to me for the last time to ask me to come back to me. "I am a married man, and I need my family." He had been gone for almost a year.

I didn't answer him but instead looked at the woman across the building from me. She was one of the Jewish inhabitants living and dying on the Lower East Side. She was reaching out for some fruit left on the shelf of her windowsill. And I understood everything then, absolutely everything: that I had lived and would die alone, but that I would be better off clinging to the belief that someone would save me. Indeed, Jose was not going to save me when he was himself so insane. And I turned back to him and told him he needed medical help. Jose left. The fact was that I had begun on a new journey in my life, and I didn't need him anymore. He belonged to the past.

Chapter 18: Memories of My Children

I had finished my first year at Old Westbury and returned for my second.

Brooke was born and just a few months old when I put her into the daycare center at Old Westbury. Barbara Ehrenreich was also involved with the center as her daughter went there. I wish I could say I did the right thing, but I didn't. Putting Brooke in daycare so young just alienated her from me and made her distant and far removed. I would visit her at the center between classes, but it differed from paying attention to her. I would drop her off at the center and, after classes, pick her up again. I had a car that I owned with a friend of mine. I could use it during the week, and he used it during the weekend to drive his family around. We paid for everything, half- and- half. [1] I dropped Tiel off at Children's Welcome, and I would drive out to Old Westbury, which was a very long drive, drop Brooke off at daycare, and then spend the rest of the day having classes, pick her up, and drive to Manhattan again. I would pick up Tiel, go home, cook dinner, wash my children, and put them to bed. Then I would begin to study.

Tiel at least had me for a long enough time to bind to me, but poor Brooke was a lost soul. Moreover, Tiel was beginning to show signs of mental illness as well. When she was very young, at around a year or so, I tried to teach her phonics, but she showed no interest. I wanted to teach her how to count, but she refused. The only thing I could teach her was art, which I did at a young age. At the age of one year, she started painting and never really stopped being an artist. It was in her. But she was not inclined to learn anything else.

When she was three, a few months before Brooke was born, she came to me and told me that she wanted another mother. I looked at her, astounded. "What do you mean you want another mother." "I want her to be like Debbie Takis," she said. Debbie Takis was one of the women in the daycare center Tiel went to. She was a friend of mine, and we had dinner together, at my house or hers. "Why." She answered that I didn't dress like the people on T.V. I was so upset that after I put her to bed, I called Beth Israel Medical Center and spoke to a psychiatrist. They were kind enough to get me one, who told me that they had a Medical Center where I could take her to find out what was wrong with her and why she felt that way.

I took her to the clinic for a long time, and they told me nothing; I got tired after going there for so long. They weren't about to give me a diagnosis. But I knew there was something wrong with her. It would take a long time to find out what, nearly forty years of her life.

I had graduated from Old Westbury. We did not wear caps and gowns at graduation because it would separate us from the people. I am trying to remember who the speaker was for the graduation, but I do know that he made us promise that wherever we saw people's suffering, we should rise to the occasion. Marilyn and her wonderful husband, Larry, came to watch. Brooke was there, and Tiel.

Marxism was a way of presenting myself. My psychopathy, which was still quite hidden from me, nonetheless remained, and this offered me a much more acceptable way to respond to those around me. I had no feelings for "people," but I could respond to the abstract people of the revolution. I had developed a social conscience that was not natural but only mimicked other people's values of what a good society should be like. I was on my way to becoming a teacher: a people-mover. That is what mattered to me: having power over others while making them think I cared about them.

I won a scholarship to study women's studies at Sarah Lawrence. I was so excited to be able to attend. I could take my children with me and have a house on campus. I went up there to be interviewed by the head of the department. That shattered my dreams. Her name was Gerda Lerner, and she told me, point blank, that I had not graduated from a university. After all, Old Westbury had only been open for a few years, and most of my teachers were not Ph. D.s, not prepared to teach college. Look at my professors, Diedre English and Barbara Ehrenreich; who were they, and what were their qualifications? She told me that even though the college had accepted me, she hadn't, and if I came there to study, I would be miserable under her tutelage.

I decided not to go. It wasn't just Dr. Lerner's complaints; I also had to leave New York and the Lower East Side. The question was, what was I going to do? Of course, without the Old Westbury money, I now found myself living off of Welfare. That was no way to live; I received enough money for rent, food, and little else.

Chapter 19: Memories of Larry and Bart

Marilyn was the woman whom Cory got involved with when we broke up. She was a redhead with a cute face and a wonderful talent for dancing. After nearly a year of putting up with Cory's abuse, she got pregnant. She was hoping that Cory would change once the baby was born. Not. She would eventually leave him after he started abusing the young infant. less than six months old, because he was a "mama's boy." I don't remember how I got in touch with Marilyn again as I was breaking up with Jose, but she lent me the money so I could get my own apartment and helped me get into Children's Welcome, and we became friends. We used to spend weekends together, she with her son, Kevin, and I with my daughter, Tiel. We would wander through the East or West Village, where she lived. Much of our time was spent around Washington Square, watching our kids play in the park and discussing old and new times. Most of the time, we got uproariously stoned and sat around giggling. We ate huge amounts of candy to satisfy our munchies. We laughed at life.

We also had wonderful times with the women from the cooperative daycare center. Marilyn had come down with liver disease and could not work for months and was likewise living off of welfare. All of us were poor women who had children and, for one reason or another, left our husbands or lovers or had them leave us. We were working women who struggled to survive and lived on the brink of poverty. Once a week, we would gather together and have dinner. Each of us would "appropriate" food from the stores and bring it to dinner. One woman had a real gift for this and so liberated "Pate de foie gras" and fine cheeses, and we would chip in for a few bottles of wine, and no one lived better than us. There was a Christmas when we had no money, so we appropriated gifts for our children. I remember Brooke got a portable fish tank, which allowed her to sit and watch the fish swimming. There were presents for Kevin and Tiel, and all this was thanks to Marilyn. We took care of each other's children when we needed to go out, not just in the daycare center but in general. We watched out for one another, and it was a remarkable experience for how we shared our lives. I look back on this as if it were the best days of my life: I had children but no husband to answer to. I was studying at Old Westbury and was learning about the lies I had been told about America: how it really wasn't the best country in the world, how Socialism was better. I had good friends from the daycare cooperative and Marilyn, who helped and whom I helped at every point in my life. This was a lesson in liberation, and I was, at least for the time being, becoming more liberated. I was the least narcissistic I had ever been. I was a communal human being in a communal society, and the effects, in the short term, were amazing. I was less of a psychopath, less of a narcissist than I had ever been.

When Children's Welcome was funded under the poverty program, everything changed. Sherry and Erinie had no qualifications as teachers and had to leave, and we got two teachers with a background in Early Childhood Education. In addition to my going on board as a part-time chef, we also hired a substitute teacher by the name of Larry Davis. He was wonderful and patient with the children; we thought we were lucky to have him. It was with Larry Davis that Marilyn fell in love. At that time, however, he was married to a Colombian woman named Isabell. After their wedding, he went to Colombia for a celebration with her family. However, no sooner had she gotten back than she received a message that her mother was very ill, so she went home to take care of her. Larry, who was running out of money, could do nothing but sit and wait for her.

In time, he and Marilyn became involved with one another and fell in love. He said when he met Marilyn and looked at her, he knew she was "the one". They decided to continue the affair until his wife came back, and then they would end it. His wife was gone for almost a year before she wrote that she was coming home. It seemed like the relationship between Marilyn and Larry was destined to end. Isabella had a surprise for Larry. She told him that she had fallen in love with another man and that she wanted a divorce. In fact, she had married Larry to get her papers deliberately, and now that the year was up, she could find someone else and still have her citizenship, or so she thought. She was dead wrong. Marilyn and Larry were very happy with the outcome, and soon thereafter, Larry got a divorce.

Marilyn got thrown out of her apartment because it wasn't legally hers, and they moved into an apartment just down the hall from mine. It was beautifully renovated by a woman who had lived there before: it had a raised area for eating, a fireplace, which she had discovered and renovated, and a large, open area. There was a room for Kevin as well.

We had a wonderful time together. We used to take turns making dinner and eating it with some fine and not so fine wine. We took our children to the pools opened by the city, and Larry would hold Brooke and twirl her around. Kevin and Tiel played together. We went to the Village, East and West. Occasionally, we had breakfast or dinner in one of the local Ukrainian restaurants. Larry and Marilyn went out dancing, and I watched the children. Being stoned, we laughed a lot. We were very much a family.

Larry was a tall, thin, light-skinned Black man. He came from a background that should have produced a narcissist but instead produced a kind and gentle person who deeply cared for other people. He had a mother who suffered from chronic heart disease and had been in a mental institution throughout her life because she was schizophrenic. She had a child when she was younger, a daughter, and went for a long time before she became pregnant again with one of the patients in a mental institution where she was staying and gave birth to her second child, Larry. His life, or most of it, was spent taking care of his mother, who had to be turned over in the middle of the night so she could breathe. He was, in a sense, the child who took care of the mother and not the other way around. He was looking, of course, for a woman who would take this burden from him and allow him to be a child, telling him what to do and how to do it. He found her in Marilyn.

The thing I loved most about Larry was that he was endlessly curious. He had no higher education but had a deep interest in whatever I was studying at Old Westbury and saw it as an opportunity to learn. No matter what I was reading, he was interested in talking about it, and we had long discussions over issues that most people didn't care about. Sometimes, he became very interested in a book I was reading, so he borrowed it from me to read. One book was Engels "Origin of the Family, Private Property and the State. " He was going to read it, and we were going to talk about it. He had the book on his desk when another hospital worker stopped and was shocked. "You are reading this book"? It was indeed a strange book for Larry to be reading. He introduced himself to Larry and said to him that he had read this book as part of a course in Marxist Theory. They became fast friends and often went into the bathroom to smoke Marijuana. Larry told this man about me, and he also came home and told me about this guy whose name was Bart. "Oh, Larry, I am not really interested in meeting this guy or any other guy I said." "No, you are really going to like him. He is also reading The Origins of the Family, Private Property, and The State. He's a very interesting person." I arranged to meet the man named Bart Metzger who was so interested in socialism.

I was shocked by his appearance when I walked into the house to meet Bart. He had hair down past his shoulders and was very, very thin. He looked like John Lennon from the Beetles and had glasses that reinforced the image. Oh my God, a hippie, I thought. We started discussing revolution and China, and I found him very interesting. I enjoyed the meeting and the conversation but didn't expect to meet him again as he was going out to California. A few days later, I was sitting at my new job at New York University, and I lifted my head to find Bart. He had come to ask me out for lunch, and I became interested in having another fascinating conversation about Marx.

We talked about so many exciting things: the revolution and Marxism, and also what he was doing, which was studying Marxism with a Professor at New York University, Bertell Ollman. He could not stop talking about Bertell. I told him I had started a course at New School in psychology but quit because it was very unfulfilling for me. He asked me if I would like to go with him to hear Bertell speak, and of course, I said yes.

I went to New York University to meet Bart and Bertell. Bart first response was to point to a woman in an inappropriate fashion pointing out that she had been interested in him. This was to make me jealous, but I felt no jealousy. Then, Professor Ollman came in and started to talk about dialectical materialism, and I sat there mesmerized. It seemed to me as though his mind glowed because of all the wisdom he possessed. I can't say I understood much of what he said because I didn't, but I understood that what he was saying was so important to me that I had to learn it.

Without an appointment, I met him at the Politics Department the next day. I walked in and introduced myself, and I told him that it didn't matter whether I was a matriculated or non-matriculated student; I wanted to study with him. I wanted this more than anything because I was a Marxist and needed to learn Dialectics with him. I needed it the way I need the air I breathe. He listened to me and said he would see what he could do. In a week, I received a letter from New York University that I had been accepted into the program for a master's degree in Politics. However, it came with the stipulation that I had to maintain a B+ conditional to stay in. It didn't matter because now I would study with Bertell and learn everything one had to learn to think dialectically. I was so thrilled.

Bart continued to come to my apartment. He was a vegetarian, just like me, and I made him dinners, and we ate, then sat around and talked. The intensity of his intellectual passions impressed me more than anything else. He was a "class act"; not merely the revolutionary ideals we had learned at Old Westbury, but the educated mind of an educated person. He spoke, and I understood everything I had to learn; I understood everything Gerda Lerner told me about what it means to be truly educated. I understood why I could not understand Bertell. I understood why I had to read Marx twice or thrice to know what he was saying. Whenever I looked at Bart, he expressed the fine finesse of his ideas. I wanted to speak with the confidence with which he spoke, to use his vocabulary, and to be as confident and self-assured as he was. It was not Bart I wanted; it was Bart's mind. I wanted to become him.

Bart had other ideas. I saw him as an intellectual to whom I aspired; he saw me as a woman he wanted to sleep with. He was a man with a passion for me. I remember looking one night and seeing the lust in his eyes, and I didn't know what the hell I was going to do about this. He told me afterward that he would leave me and move on if he didn't get what he wanted very soon. Our friendship meant nothing to him.

One night he came to my house. He used to ride his bicycle from his apartment to mine, and it was raining very hard on this particular night. It was so hard I didn't feel he could ride his bike in the rain and suggested to him that he might sleep over. He said yes, and I asked him where he wanted to sleep, and he said with me, and I knew that I had to go ahead and make this a sexual relationship if I was going to keep him. And so, we slept together. Afterward, he would say to me that he had never really slept with a woman before. He was seven years younger than me and, of course, had never slept with a real woman before.

He was just 20, and I was 27

Chapter 20: Memories of Bart

His Father, Norman Metzger, lived his life for this boy. He could do no wrong, and he tried his best to give him, physically and mentally, everything he wanted. There was no thought that this was not good for him in the end, that giving him what he wanted contributed to his narcissism and self-indulgence. Nothing matters but what you want, most generally caused by indulgent parents. In turn, Norman was himself a narcissist who received this treatment from his father, who thought of him as the king of the world. It didn't matter that Norman had a sister, as she was irrelevant in his and his father's eyes, or that he had a wife, whom he cheated on incessantly; the only thing that mattered was his son, his pride, and his joy.

Bart had gone to college and taken a year off to travel the world. He went to Amsterdam as it was the pot capital of the world. Bart imagined that he would become a writer and spend his time writing, smoking pot, and then looking at pastries in coffee shops' windows but never buying them. He was, you see, quite chubby at this time, and it was crucial to him to lose this weight and become as thin as he could. It was Bart's way of overcoming his mother's obsession with feeding him fattening foods when he was little. It was also his way of becoming like his skinny Father. He looked at the pastries and then went home and weighed himself on the scale, so happy that he was losing weight at an enormous rate.

He made money by shipping pot home to his friends. And he made a lot of money, which he, in turn, used to buy more pot for himself. He would ship them in the empty entrails of stuffed animals and say your Teddy Bear has arrived; that is how sloppy the Postal Service was in those days.

He decided to take a trip and go down to the hashish capital of the world, Morocco. In Morocco, men would sit in tea houses, bombed out of their minds, looking at large-screen televisions. While Bart was there, he became friendly with someone who wanted to invite him back to his house to smoke hashish. However, that was not what his friend had in mind. Soon after, they wandered off the beaten path and into a part of the city Bart wasn't familiar with. He attempted to rape Bart. I don't know whether Bart got away or did not, but he no longer loved the freedom of being alone. Nearly emaciated by his desire to lose weight, his hair long now, he went home to his parents in New York and enrolled at New York University, where he studied when I first met him.

His parents were only so glad to have him back, at least his mother was. Marcia was still dressing him under the covers. He was almost twenty, and his mother was dressing him under the covers. I don't want to tell you how strange this was. Norman began to see the flaws in Marcia's relationship with her son and wanted him out. Not just for his relationship with his mother but because he continued to smoke pot and for this reason, if not for anything else, his father wanted him far away from home in case he got busted. Norman fed up with it, put his foot down, and Bart got an apartment on the Lower East Side, close to New York University.

Marcia still performed all her tasks on the Lower East Side. Norman and Marcia both indulged Bart but in different ways. She rode down to meet him, bought him clothes, cooked dinners, and cleaned. Bart lived alone, but that old tie between Mother and Son still held sway. He was still Mama and Papa's "sunny" when I met him, and this would never change.

Such was the state of the Bart I knew. Indulged by his father and taken care of by his mother, he was a spoiled child who pretended all the while to be a Marxist hippy who was surviving all alone. I was not surprised that he had flunked kindergarten because of his tantrums. He threw a tantrum if the car in front of him stopped, if he could not find his wallet, if the elevator did not come on time, for any reason.

MEMORIES OF A PSYCHOPATH

When I came into his life with my two children, he saw me as a substitute for his mother, and he responded by calling me "Mama" as if I had no identity of my own. I accepted this, at least initially, because I felt him to be intellectually superior to me. He used to go to Paul Stewart with his Father to buy his clothes, but I soon went along, picking out what he wanted. I never got anything for myself. I was always the "poor relative" of the group, as, for that matter, was his mother. Our relationship was to serve the men and care for their needs, our own being unimportant. This was a world that revolved around men.

He didn't let me know until I was pregnant with our daughter Erica, but he had rape fantasies that filtered through his mind. He had no interest in coming but only in staying in me for as long as possible, living out the fantasy of a raped woman. Once Erica was born, what he wanted became more evident to me, and I stopped sleeping with him. I tried to leave him at that point, but I could not with three children. Smoking marijuana was a regular part of our relationship. We lived constantly being stoned, day and night, which led me to live amid my misery in a euphoric high. The only way I could deal with him was while I was stoned.

We got married in upstate New York at the holiday home of Bart's parents. It was located on a lake, and one day, just before the wedding, my father-in-law asked me to go fishing with him. I was shocked because he never asked me to go anywhere with him. We were moving in the right direction, becoming more of a father/daughter relationship, and so I was happy to go along. When we got out into the lake, he turned to me and told me a story. "There was this rich Jewish woman who had a son. One day, she was going out to get a cab, and a man followed her, carrying the son. The doorman, new to the job, asked her, 'Oh, what is wrong with you son? He can't walk." She turned around, looked at him, and said, "And why should he." With that, my father-in-law returned to shore, and I learned my lesson. I was marrying a man whose mother would ask why he should walk when he didn't have to and whose father agreed with her. They would stand by their son and indulge his every wish as long as they could. I, in turn, would be there to service him in all the ways they couldn't.

We got married the next day at the shore of the lake. There was a justice of the peace, and the children were there. I am trying to remember who else witnessed us. There is a picture of me, dressed in old white blouse and white slacks, standing there, looking content. I felt that I would win in this battle between his parents and myself. I was, after all, his wife, and I said to him that afternoon that he would change now, becoming my husband and not his parents' child. He looked at me and said nothing. It was never going to happen. He would always belong to his parents first and to me second.

We had the reception for the wedding a day later at Marcia's house. Everyone who came to the wedding was a friend of Marcia' except for Marilyn and Larry and my Aunt Bertha. My Aunt looked at Bart in an armchair in the living room and said, "I don't know how you managed to get him." No one congratulated me on my marriage. No one congratulated the two of us.

Very soon after, I got pregnant. We went to Bart's parents to tell them. Marcia's response was to tell us to get an abortion. We went home in a rage because she said this. A few weeks later, his father asked me whether I thought it would be a boy or a girl. As I said, we did not know then, and I told him so. However, I thought it might be a girl, as I usually give birth to girls. He looked at me and said, "Well, we give birth to sons, and I think it will be a boy." He was waiting for the third installment of the Metzger family of men. They would worship and adore the son of his "sunny" in the bond of paternal bliss.

Erica was born on August 1st. She had red hair and blue eyes and looked as much like my family as you could imagine. Bart's family was dark-haired and dark-eyed, and Erica did not resemble them. I called Bart after she was born and said what beautiful hands she had, precisely like a piano player. I also commented on how, when they brought her to me, Erica lifted herself and looked at me. She seemed so strong. But there was almost no response from the Metzger's on the birth of their child, and I began to wonder. All that would end when they decided that an aunt in their family had red hair, although no blue eyes. This was proof that I had not cheated on Bart and that this was his baby. But there was a grave disappointment in his heart and his father's heart that I had not had a son. Marcia alone embraced the child as if it were hers; she took great joy in her. It was almost as if she had a son and now a daughter, both of whom she would raise as she saw fit. I was, in turn, the woman who would change the child, feed it, and then return to Marcia to play with. It was hardly the relationship I wanted with Erica, but it was the relationship that existed between Grandmother and Granddaughter, which I could never break. Erica remained her grandmother's child until her grandmother died. She was never mine.

Of course, by the time Erica was born, Bart was no longer a student at New York University. He had set off on the road to become his Father. At around 23, just having finished his master's degree at N.Y.U., he abruptly gave up his plans to become a college professor and joined his father in becoming a hospital administrator. Because of his Father's connections, he was given the role of Human Resources Director at Bellevue Hospital. From that day onward, he was to stay in various roles as the direct human resources at several other hospitals in New York, Washington D.C., Pittsburgh, and, finally, Boston. He looked increasingly like his Father with a heavy mustache, a small, thin frame, and a passion for dressing in Paul Stewart clothing. He was the image of Norman Metzger in his mind and soul, and aside from the fact that he was far less stable and more emotional than his Father, he continued in his Father's profession.

Our marriage was likewise unfolding. When Bart stopped wanting to be a college professor, I felt my dreams going down the drain. I, meanwhile, was continuing at New York University, struggling to become an instructor. I had taken my B plus conditional and gotten straight A's. This, in turn, made the University give me a full scholarship. When I was pursuing my Ph.D., I was honored to receive a Helbein Fellowship, which paid my tuition and gave me extra money to pursue to do whatever I wanted. I got a fellowship, not approved but granted by H. Mark Roeloffs, to teach his classes as well. I graded papers for him and watched him advise his students. From this man who had been voted Teacher of the Year so many times, I learned to teach Politics and how to have students learn to write papers.

I got teaching work at Rutgers University before I got my Masters' Degree. Then I got a job at Kean University, where I taught American Government and Comparative Politics. I had a bright future ahead of me, or so I thought. Moreover, I now spoke like an educated person. I no longer envied Bart for his academic way of talking. I didn't envy him at all anymore.

With the birth of Erica, as with so many marriages, our relationship also began to fail. Bart no longer had the patience for my children. He became abusive to them. To Tiel, less so, because she was just too beautiful, everything was forgiven, but to Brooke, Bart was the cruelest of all. He punished her often by slapping her on the head. He persecuted her for the slightest thing. I, of course, began to argue with him over this and, finally, threatened him. It created a barrier between us that was insurmountable. Mine was a family that was divided from the beginning.

I no longer slept with him and went to bed as if I were hiding from him, in layer after layer of clothing, the last one being a short jacket zipped up the front. We never had sex. Perhaps in response, or maybe it was one of his rape fantasies, he began by cutting out pictures from girly magazines and hiding them all over the apartment. They were under the rugs in the wall-to-wall carpeting I had in the bathroom; I found the cutout legs of a woman in his shorts just taken from the wash. I went to work and asked to borrow his as his briefcase, a lot of copies to give to my students. When I opened them, pictures of women fell out. At each point, I threatened him with this. His response was to tell me that they weren't his. That someone had come into the apartment and left them there. When I found them in the children's room, I told him I would have to go if this didn't stop.

It seemed as though he had stopped. They were gone, or so I thought. I went to have dinner with Bart at his office, and he was late as he was in a meeting. I turned to one of his files, in which he included all kinds of information about political struggles in the world. A thick folder was between the People's Republic of China and Vietnam. I opened it up, and it was filled with pictures of women's genitalia. He had not stopped; he had just moved his collection to his office. I didn't confront him because there was no use in confronting him; this was a habit. Instead, I dropped the folders between the files and the wall in the back of them. When Bart came, I went to dinner with him and never mentioned anything. I noticed how anxious he had gotten when he knew they were gone. It wasn't until about a year later that Bart told me they were coming in to paint his room, and then I told him where they were. "I wondered where they were he said," and that was it.

I was waiting to get my Ph.D. and leave him—just another few months at best. Bart, who perhaps had known this, got out first. We had gone to a party at a hospital he worked at. It was aboard a ship sailing from Manhattan's shore out the Statue of Liberty. After we spent a few hours there dancing and drinking, we would return to shore.

There, I noted Abigail Abysahl, the woman who was to become his lover and long-time wife. At first, I didn't think anything of her. Here I was, his slim wife with a charming personality. Abbey looked like a ship. She had long hair that she wore so that it covered her face. Abbey was immense, I mean very large. She had nothing about her that made her appealing, well, nothing but one thing: she loved Bart. While we were sitting around the room, Abbey told him, in front of this enormous group of people, that she did love him. She said this out loud so that everyone could hear. I was a little taken aback but thought that this woman could not hold a candle to me. I was so wrong. To someone hungry for love, she was the respite.

A few days later, Bart came to drop off Erica at N.Y.U., and as he walked around to open the door and let her out, he turned to me and said, "You don't love me, do you." I said nothing at all. That was the end of our marriage. He was moving to Washington, D.C., to be a hospital administrator there. I stayed behind at New York University to finish my degree, and Abbey was visiting Bart in D.C.

I still need to finish my doctorate; having completed my comprehensives: I need to finish my Ph.D. dissertation. I was now financially responsible for caring for my children again and did not know what to do.

Chapter 21: Memories of The Divorce

My divorce was a combination of a more or less sense of freedom from the day-to-day hatreds of the person we were married to, and at the same time, a longing for a new start. It is also, the ending of something known and familiar and the peering out into a future that was uncertain. For me it represented a long slow deterioration of my marriage dysfunction marriage, that ended not with Bart leaving, but with the sure, firm knowledge that I would return to my original state of being alone. Not just being alone, but at the same time, being responsible for my children once again. They would, of course, suffer the consequence of our divorce, each of them dealing with Bart's absence in a different way. For Tiel, it came at a time when she was almost grown, and so felt the absence of a father as a freedom to go ahead and do what she wanted to do. There was no Bart to protect her from the world. Brooke was only too glad to know that he was gone. She was free from his abuse and spent much of her time watching TV and not doing anything in school. Erica was lost without her father, and so pulled away from us as a group and began to find her fulfillment in her friends and Bart's family. I was more alone than I had ever been, unable to repair this distance between my children and myself. I had been so caught up in my hatred of my husband, and in my days of glory at New York University that they were pushed to the background and survived on their own. In truth, I was not paying attention to anything but the relief from Bart and the worry about what my future without him would be like. In general, we had put up with his tantrums and fantasies, only to find out that he was gone, and nothing we put up with mattered. It was a gesture in futility.

I paid little attention to anything aside from ruminating about the past and worrying about the future. I had been teaching an honors course in the expository writing program at New York University and spent the summer working on it. I would be a study of the ways in which an exploited people were discriminated against; political exclusions, economic subservience, and finally, the threat of violence to be used to keep them in their places. In it I would show that exploitation was the same regardless of whether one was a woman, or black, or a member of the working class or an exploited minority such as gays. I had my students read Karl Marx, Malcolm X, The Color Purple, and another book about gay youths. This was in 1975.

But a little while after I began teaching it, I found I was too distracted to teach at all. I walked in one day and said to my students that it was not I but they who were going to teach this class; that each student was to write a paper about exploitation and how they had suffered from it and read it to the class and on that basis, I would give my grade. This turned out to be a lesson in how students could teach one another far better than any teacher. As they sat there and discussed their exploitation, I sat and listened and learned far more than I could teach. My first student talked about how she was exploited as a woman because she worked as a dancer in a club in order to get money to attend New York University. She said how degraded it made her feel that males leached after her, but how she had no choice as there was no other way for her to afford to attend such a prestigious school. She was followed by a student who appeared to be "perfect". He was handsome, well off, and suffered no consequences that were the result of poverty or exploitation. But when he spoke, he told us that despite the fact that he had never experience exploitation in the sense of a minority, he himself suffered from the consequences of being a junkie. He was, in fact, hooked on heroin. He was 17 years old.

Several students spoke of what it was like to be gay. One spoke of the constant abuse she received from her parents when she underperformed academically. Ulla spoke of the responsibilities that fell on her as the last child who was supposed to live up to her family's expectations for her, as her old sister was married. On and on it went, and I sat there and listened; we all sat there and listened and never, not ever, have I had a class open up to one another as that one did. At the end of the year, I had a party for my students. We ate and drank bottles of Champagne, and at the end of the day, we said goodbye. It was a bittersweet ending; one in which we had come together, gotten to get to know one another, and now had to move on knowing that we would forever hold one another in our hearts.

Chapter 22: Memories of Ulla

I had begun teaching at New York University the year before and had a class of primarily young American students learning to write. I did, however, have a student who was not American named Ulla Coppola de Anna.

She had gone to university in Milan and come to the United States to prepare herself for a degree in economics. She would follow in the footsteps of her father, Julian, who, like his father, was a distinguished economist. Her older sister was married and did not want to study economics but was very happy to sit at home and be a mother. It was to her the second daughter who was expected to fulfill her father's dreams in life. The problem was that she needed help learning English.

She spoke well enough to be understood but needed help to write correctly, as there were so many errors. While teaching at New York University, I had office hours, so I saw her, reviewed her papers with her, and tried to help her. I could say I paid attention to her, but I did not. She was one of many students I had to counsel, and while her writing was essential to me, it was no more or less important than the other students in my class. However, I remember one thing about her that stood out: she came up to me after every class and offered me a cigarette, as we could smoke in the university in those days. She walked with me, as other students did, as we talked about writing or politics, but I paid no attention to her. At the end of the first year, I was ready to drop her as a student in my honors class.

When she found out, she came to me and said that she wanted to study with me again as I had helped her so much with her language, and I would please allow her to attend my classes this term. I said yes, and so she came into my class not quite ready for a course on exploitation but feeling I could help her with her writing, nonetheless.

As I said, I was going through a divorce and not yet ready to deal with my students at all.

I was preoccupied and distracted and could not deal with someone else. When Ulla began to call me and ask me for advice, I told her I could not come in when she wanted me to. However, if she wanted to come to my home in New Jersey, I would give her as much help as possible. And she came.

Not long after that, I began to tell her about my divorce from Bart, and we began to talk. Well, I talked, and she listened. She listened and listened, and when it seemed she could no longer listen, she still listened. She stood by me at a time when no one else could. Her listening became like a mirror that reflected me into myself. I understood myself much better when I got done talking with her. I did not see her as a woman or even a person but as a mirror that listened to my self-musings. In turn, I helped her with her writing.

One day, when she called to come over, I was particularly depressed and asked her if we could set our meeting for another day. She responded that I sounded like I needed someone to talk to, and she was coming right over.

Now, when she came, she did not just stay for the afternoon but the whole weekend. She would take the children to concerts, or we would all ride in the afternoon in my huge van, which I named "Matilda," to see the country. We became friends, and in time, we went out for evenings together. She had some fascinating friends. One was a woman who was an expert on the financial market, and every word she said caused people to listen to her advice. She lived in a large home on Sutton Place, and we could look out across the city from her place. We went to dances in the lofts of SoHo and the Village, where exciting people were. Men used to hit on us, and we flirted with them, but at the end of the evening, we went home together.

I had been with Bart for so long that I had forgotten what it was like to go out dancing. She had friends worldwide, and life became exciting because of Ulla.

Ulla was also there when it came to dealing with Bart. On one occasion, he called to ask me to meet him so he could discuss my failings as a mother. That was what it was about. I needed to take the garbage out more efficiently. I was not harping on the children because of their homework. That, and a thousand other things, was what Bart had to talk to me about.

Ulla agreed that she would go with me to meet him. It was a good idea as I could not deal with him alone. I met her in the city and waited for her to get dressed so we could go. She began to get dressed in a sexy outfit. "What are you doing? Are you thinking of coming on to my husband?" which was the only way I could view this situation. She did not say one word as we got ready to go.

When we got to the bar, he was waiting for us. He began by reciting everything I had to do that I wasn't doing. Ulla just sat there, and before I could answer, she responded, "Well, what are you doing about it? The children are your responsibility, too," and he didn't know what to say. Without raising her voice or getting into an argument with him, she stated the simple facts: that the children were not just my responsibility but his, and what would he do about their problems? I would have defended myself, but she put him in a position of defending himself, and he shut up, looked at her, and did not say one word.

We decided to drive him home, before Ulla went to my place. Before she could do this, she would call her boyfriend because there were no mobile phones in those days. She exited "Matilde" and walked to the phone booth, and Bart commented on how beautifully she walked. Without thinking about it, I said, "Don't think about it because she is mine." I was shocked by what I said. I could not believe it. Bart understood immediately that we, at least at some level, belonged to one another. She was mine in a sense I didn't understand. I was, after all, a straight woman, and she lived with a man, and so our feelings were loving but without love.

That is what I said to myself. Ulla was, without question, one of the most beautiful women I have ever met. She was, like her mother, Scandinavian in appearance with long auburn hair and blue eyes. Her skin was fair, not dark like her swarthy father, and she looked like she belonged in one of the pictures of Roman women painted by Lawrence Alma-Tadema, the one with the red hair looking up into the admiring gaze of her darker companions.

She came one day when I was having dinner with my friends and ate with us. When she finished, she decided to walk with the children while I cleaned up and made coffee for my friend Sidel. Sidel, who was much older than I and had had a far more interesting life when it came to sexual matters, said to me. "Oh, you know that young girl has a crush on you.

I could see how, she looked at you." I had no idea, and it didn't matter because, as I said, that "was part of being their teacher; they had crushes on me, and I could not act on it."

And that was that. We were still friends; she was still my student, and I was to behave honorably. But the thought stayed in my mind; it did, and I could not get over the fact that she had a crush on me. And I grew close to her.

On that evening, when my students came to say a last goodbye to me, I was sitting on the bench just watching everyone do what they were doing. I loved these students so much. And while I was there, Ulla came to sit next to me, leaned herself against me, and said like a whisper in a dream, "Well, we are not students and teachers anymore," and I understood what she and I had been waiting for. It did not happen soon, but it did happen as our love for each other grew. At first, spending time with her was just a continuous joy. One evening, we went out to enjoy the Festivities at the Feast of San Gennaro, and I longed for her without question. I had to tell her just how much she meant to me.

At last, we sat down to have a drink, and I was about to tell her when she abruptly said, "What do you think Bart will say? She asked me. "Say about what I asked?" "That you and I love each other." She said it all; everything I felt and sensed, she said it. We did not make love right then and there. She lived with a boyfriend on East 20th Street and so went home to where he was and slept. However, we went to my bedroom the next time she came to my house. It was pouring rain out, and I started to tell her what she meant to me. She got up, took her clothes off, and said to me. "Just do whatever you want," and our first, somewhat awkward lovemaking began. We touched each other gently, and I slowly went down to where she was sensitive. She came so quickly that I was shocked. Well, I said to myself, we did want each other. But this was an ongoing thing, and I had to come first before she engaged in her orgasmic fireworks.

When I awoke in the morning, she was already up and down in the kitchen, telling her boyfriend about what had happened. I could not believe my ears and said to her as if I had done something wrong, as if I had been the aggressor, that I was sorry, that I didn't mean for it to happen. But it did happen, over and over again. First, the relapse into passion, then her regret, and my apologies, and then we would do it again. In the end, I finally said to her that I would sleep with her if she wanted me to or not sleep with her. But I could not go on like this; I could not do something I wanted to and then find myself apologizing. We continued to make love without her talking about it any further.

It was new to me, and I did not understand what it was supposed to be like.

Bart and I had always had sadomasochistic straight sex, with none of the gentleness and kindness I had gotten from Ulla. We lived out the rape fantasy, and I never did realize that there was another, softer version of the whole thing. But even though Ulla was kind and gentle with me, there was an element to her I did not understand. When it was over, it was over, and there was none of the postal coital bliss present either. And this, I did not understand at all.

By the end of June, she was returning to Rome, and I had accepted that I might see her again in the fall. We were sitting at a bar one day when she turned and said to me that her parents wanted me to come to Rome to thank me for all I had done for Ulla. I looked at her, and she was smiling. And so it was that I got my flight and went to Rome sometime in late May.

She met me at the airport, and we went high up into the city to see all of Rome.

I was so happy despite my jet lag, and we kissed and looked at the city. We went home, and we made love after I slept for a while. There wasn't anything more beautiful than romance in Rome.

But it was all so strange. Not because it was Rome but because of Ulla. We would go out to eat but always at some bad area. To be sure, the food was great and so I didn't think anything of it. At times, we would stop, and she would get out of the car and tell me she would be right back and go over into another vehicle. She would stay there for a while, sometimes half an hour, and then return. This was, ostensibly, to buy pot or hash. When we went back to her apartment, we would go lay down on her bed, smoke a joint, and make love. This one evening, she rolled a joint for us, and as she did so, her bracelets, which she always wore, fell back, and I could see the hug puncture on her wrist. Then, I understood everything. She was going into the car not to buy pot, which would have taken only a second, but to shoot up heroin. Suddenly, all the things she had shown herself to be the silent partner who listened but did not speak; the woman who moved as if she were in a dream and not part of reality, as Bart had noted; the intense sex drive, the slowness, the laziness, all fell into place. I looked at her and her arm, and she just laughed. "I am a junkie she said." She said this as if she had said something amusing that I would laugh at, too.

I looked at her and thought of how I could have gotten Aids, and I stood up and said to her, "If I don't have it by now, I consider myself lucky. But I will never sleep with you again." And that was it. She tried a few days later, but I was finished with her. I got home to the US and had an Aids test. It was negative. But I still had to wait to see if I got it. In about a year, I was sure that I did not. In the meantime, I started Ki Foods and began the next chapter of my life.

She would occasionally come to me and lay in bed with me. I let her come, but I never touched her again sexually. It was as if some memory, some dream, haunted us and brought us together, but I was not going to sleep with her. Then, she went away for about a year before I heard from her again. She called and asked if I could stop by her apartment; she wanted to speak to me.

When I got there, she talked about the fact that she was sick, that she thought it was her liver, and what she could do. Her boyfriend twitched because if she had it, he had it, no question about it. I told her I had no idea what she could do.

And I left.

Chapter: 23: Memories of Ki Foods

My contract at the university was over, and if I stayed any longer, I would have a tenure-line job, which wasn't permitted. I had not looked for anything else, as I had too much to worry about. How to support the kids was a real issue for me. In addition, I had to sell the house I was living in.

I had agreed with Bart that if I got the house as my own, I would only file for child support and no marital support. Selling the home was far more complex than I could imagine. I had one buyer who wanted a new roof over the library area. Since this was a minor request, a little over 1000 dollars for the part of the roof that needed repair, I would do it. I started getting estimates. The first person who showed up had done the roof on my friend's house. I opened the door, and he looked at me and asked if I was Max. No, I said to him, my name is

Mary. Then, it dawned on us that he was reading Mary as Max, and we started laughing. His name was Kevin Finn. His estimate was better than others, and I hired him to repair the roof. In the process, we became lovers. Just that, lovers. In truth, it bored me to make love to him, even though he was a lovely person.

After my affair with Ulla, everything about sleeping with a man was a little boring for me. However, he also played the macho role to Bart, which was very important. He came and sat in the room while Bart was there and threatened him with his presence. He was a roofer, a man who worked with his back and had nothing but contempt for Bart, who was thin and wiry but, at the same time, had neither strength nor energy of my grandfather.

Since he was engaged to Abigail, Bart did not pick up Tiel or Brooke. They had no part in his life, and he felt no obligation to care for them. Bart barely spoke to them. When he decided to marry Abigail, he explained to Tiel that she and Brooke would only upset the wedding, and they were not invited, just like that. When Bart visited, he would pick up Erica, not the other children. It was as if he had never been their father for 13 years. I was heartbroken for them. What had they done to deserve this? Bart had not only divorced me, but he had also abandoned them as well, and it was cruel to both of them.

My affair with Max began when he started the roof and ended shortly after. He was a respite from Ulla, whom I longed for but would never be in a relationship with again. The sale of the house fell through, and there I was, getting ready for a new set of buyers with new demands. I knew that after the house was sold, I would have to worry about work, but it seemed very unimportant to me at this time. It was good enough that I woke up, cared for the kids, and then went to sleep again.

Bart and I were vegetarian and then vegan for our 12 years together. In my spare time when I was married, I began to take lessons in vegan cooking and Macrobiotics. In all due modesty, I consider myself one of the best vegan cooks in New York City at that time, although I did what I did for the benefit of my family and not for any other reason.

Even when Bart and I separated, I continued with Macrobiotic and Vegan cooking, as it was a part of my life. So it was that I went shopping at my local health food store to buy what I needed for dinner when I heard the following conversation between the chef and the owners of the store: "You see, my hands are so eaten by this rash that I cannot continue to cook." The owner was distraught. "But what am I going to do? Who is going to make food for my restaurant"? There was a restaurant to the right of the store, which did a pretty brisk business. I went over to the owner, whose name was Gary. His claim to fame was that he had written a song called "So Happy Together." He was a stoner and didn't care much about his health food store, even though it was successful. He made enough money from the royalties from his song and sat around the store reading the newspaper. I said, "Gary, I know how to do this cooking and can help you until you find someone else. He looked at me. "You know how to do this cooking." Yes, I am an expert Vegan cook, I told him. I will help you until you find someone else." And so, I came to work at Aquarius for the grand sum of $7.00 an hour. I only expected to be there briefly, so it didn't matter. Little did I know that it would be the beginning of Ki Foods.

I had been working there for only a short period, a week or two when I saw the possibilities. Of course, my food was far superior to the other chefs, and the clients responded by buying more and more of it. Soon, I had customers coming to me who wanted Macrobiotic Food delivered to their homes. I also began to get clients who wanted me to cook food for them. I had requests for Macrobiotic cakes with no sugar. I had a booking for a Vegan wedding, all within just a few weeks and I was beginning to make far more than the $7.00 that Gary paid me. I was making over 1,000 dollars a week.

I took out an ad in the paper, asking Gary, of course, who was too stoned to care, if I could use his address to advertise my cooking. He could care less. The Board of Health called to check up on me, and I said that I was cooking out of Gary's kitchen, and they left me alone. But the fact was that I had moved into my own house and was beginning to cook out of there.

One of my Macrobiotic customers, who lived far away in a relatively upper-middle-class neighborhood, said she often didn't eat what I had delivered. Instead of buying food from me, she wondered if I could provide it to one of the stores where she could buy it at her leisure. She had made arrangements with the store, and they were waiting for my call. Soon, I began delivering my food to another health food store, whose business grew relative to mine. The store manager went to work at an even larger store with two outlets, and I began to deliver food to them. In less than a month, I was in the health food business.

Meanwhile, the man from whom I bought tofu gave me a proposition. He used to make tofu and throw out, as a result of the process, the residue from the soybeans called okara. It was used throughout the East as a valuable addition to food, cooked into dishes, and added to baked goods to improve the product's nutritional value. But here, in America, it was regarded as waste, so he had to throw out an awful lot of okara in the process of making tofu. The bulk of his garbage was filled with okara. If I could find some use for this okara, he would give it to me for free and find a way of distributing it for me.

I played around and came up with a recipe for using it in muffins. On the other hand, oat bran was considered so valuable that it was used to make all kinds of baked products, from muffins to donuts. It was so in demand that one could not get it at all, and if one did, it was tremendously costly. I discovered that soy bran far outstripped oat bran in its nutritional value. It had linoleic acid, which gave protection against heart disease and lowered cholesterol. When I mixed the okara in the foundations for a muffin, I had an incredibly health product, which was likewise delicious. I made up a flyer with the muffins describing the health benefits and gave it to my friend to distribute. It was an instant success: I went from making two dozen in one week to over 100 dozen the next to over a thousand the following week. I could no longer cook the muffins and asked my neighbors to join me. I would mix the batter in a huge mixing bowl; my neighbors would come and pick it up and bake it, put the label on it, return it to me, and then get the next batch.

I sold the house and invested much of my money in the plant. I bought several ovens and arranged to share a space in the tofu manufacturer's plant. I was close to the source of okara, which when integrated into my baked goods, provided an accessible and inexpensive way to produce muffins. These, of course, had no sugar, eggs, or milk. They were 100% vegetarian and very, very healthy. But even as the muffins took off, so did the rest of the business. I soon had stores in New York City and Long Island. I had distributors all over the Tri-state Metropolitan area.

As I was coming home from work, I took a side street and found a caterer who had just closed. It seemed perfect, and I soon moved there with my ovens and a completely furnished kitchen. Now, I could combine my muffins and food manufacturing in one place. Less than a year after it began, my company, Ki Foods, Inc., was a major wholesaler of "gourmet foods for special diets" in New York City.

I wish I could say I arrived at some comfort with my successful business, but I did not. It consumed me, to be sure. I worked six and sometimes seven days a week, 12 to 14 hours daily. I had no partners or one to share my troubles or triumphs with. For all the years of my business, I was content to live a life of complete aloneness except for my children. I did not have a relationship, nor did I want one. I worked every day, even if I didn't have to because it was part and parcel of my life; I was Sisyphus rolling the rock up to the top of the mountain and watching it fall to earth again. When I had time with my children, I spent it going to the theatre, dinners, or indulging in their every fantasy.

Chapter 23: Memories of the Empty Nest Syndrome

In time, they left me. First came Brooke, who fell in love with a young boy in high school and continued chasing him to Pittsburgh, where she lived her life. Like me, she longed to work. Brooke had gone to a technical school where she majored in floristry. She won numerous awards but chose to work in a grocery store and a series of jobs instead. Only much later would she return to a career as a successful floral designer. She clung to her boyfriend's grandfather, praying he would return. Eventually, she moved back home and stayed with her sister until she regained her feet. But even then, she worked for minimum wage, had a series of affairs with boys she pursued long after their relationship ended, and finally met a boy named David, who broke her heart. Only after him did she decide to go back into doing floral designs and build up her career once again.

Tiel was going to school at the Fashion Institute of Technology but was constantly absorbed with boys. She was a beautiful girl who knew this. But above all else, she wanted a man to tell her that she wasn't beautiful but that she was clever, exciting, and very good at what she did. She found him. His name was Ralph, and I don't remember how they met, but I do remember that he praised her constantly for her talents, became involved in what she did and her career in design, and won her heart. She got pregnant by him and decided to keep it. They never married, but he did stay around for the baby.

He was in the Army and got out and got a job in construction. He moved in with me, and I liked Ralph, if for no other reason than the fact that he was brilliant. He had read many of the books, I had read, which was pretty amazing, which was pretty amazing because they were about politics and economics. We spent hours talking to one another about what was happening politically, the news, and the world.

All that was shot to shit when he became hooked on crack cocaine. All the fellows on the job did it, and so did he.

From the second he began taking it, he became addicted. He stole from me, his mother and father, and even his daughter, Tiel, Jr., who had been given some money for her birth. At one point, he was working at the shop with me, and I gave him my car and asked him to get some gas, come and pick us up and take us home. He was gone for hours, and we finally got a taxi to take us home. I returned to my house to find it completely stripped of anything of any value: TV sets, video equipment, even collections of coins I had inherited from my aunt, everything. It was just a matter of time until he started breaking into other people's homes and was put in jail. He would do his time, get out, and a few months later, he would be busted again for robbing someone's home and go back in.

When I was 45, I was a picture of good health and hard work. In those moments I wasn't working, I went to get a massage and treatment at an alternative health care center. I was in great shape. Then, one day, a person walked into my store and wanted to buy a box of Golden Seal tea.

I had to keep a small store open because the landlord decided I had to have retail as well as wholesale. I made quite a bit of money off this store as I sold my OK muffins and, some food we had left over from my wholesale route, and vitamins and minerals. One day, a customer stopped by to ask me for Golden Seal Tea. I had no idea what it was and told him so. He told me that it was a flush for the liver. I told him that if he came by tomorrow, I would have it for him and picked it up at one of the stores. I got one for him and one for me. The following day, I made a pot of gold seal tea and drank it, and I felt refreshed. I never drank tea, but this was great. I would begin every morning with it, as it kept me alert. But over some time, I began to feel strange from it. I stopped drinking it, but the damage was done. I felt as if there were some "insects" crawling around my gall bladder.

I told my alternative healer what I had done, and he yelled at me for drinking it. He told me that one flush was wonderful, but taking it daily ruined my gall bladder. I began to feel more pain there, and then I woke up one morning to find myself in the backyard. That's how bad the pain was. In time, I could no longer go to work, and then, I noticed my urine turning yellowish. I went to the doctor and was sent immediately to the emergency room. By the time I was admitted, I was not making any sense when I spoke; my organs were failing, and I needed massive doses of antibiotics. I remember the doctor just pushing the shunt into my body and using it to fill me full of them. In a few days, I was admitted for surgery. I had to have two surgeries. The first was to get rid of my gall bladder, and then a second in which a miniature microscope was inserted into my stomach, and the silt was removed from my liver. I had passed through the valley of the shadow of death and emerged.

My children came together to run Ki Foods for me—Brooke from Pittsburg, Tiel, who lived at my house then, and Erica. They handled the business well from beginning to end. I had no partners, but they came in and told everyone what to do and where all the food had to be delivered. They told the drivers where they had to go and counted the money when they returned. I was proud of them.

When I returned home from the hospital, I was covered with stitches and had tubes running out of me. But I was home. As I was lying on the couch talking to my children and playing with my grandchild, TJ or Tiel, Jr., Erica announced that she would live with her father. Of course, she was going on to college that year, and it was her way of announcing she would stay with Bart. It was also Bart's way of announcing that he wouldn't be spending money on child support. I let her go, knowing that she was going to go anyway. That was the last time she spent in my house. I was, and would remain, a secondary consideration for her. She used to come and visit a neighbor a few blocks away and never stopped to see me.

Tiel stayed with me for a while. But in the end, she kept returning to Ralph and Ralph's family, and in a fit of anger, I threw her out and let her go and live with them. She did for quite a while, and then I was called by the police, who said she had tried to set the house on fire with Ralph in it. I ran over and got her. I met Ralph, who was too thin from being strung out on crack. He told me I had to take her, and I did. She once again was living at my house and working with Ki Foods, and I was thrilled to have my Granddaughter living with me. I used to take her on trips to my stores, and then we would stop at some fancy restaurant for dinner. It was wonderful.

Tiel would meet Emile shortly after that, and their relationship would continue until this day, but that is another story.

When my children left, I was all alone. How one was supposed to live just for themselves alone was the question I asked. I wandered through my house, feeling the hollowness of it. I had bought it for my family, and it was now empty. To be sure, I had been a psychopath seeking my glory in the world of academia and business, but I had also provided for my family. I had, since Bart, felt myself to be the Matriarch of the Family. My children could come to me and get what they wanted materially. I provided them with their needs. Where were they now; who would I provide for?

I went through this empty nest syndrome until I realized I had to move on with my life. I still had Ki Foods. Now the question was, what would I do with my spare time? I still had TJ for most weekends. We used to love to go and visit Indian Pow Wows, which showed Native American Dancers. We used to go apple picking and pumpkin picking. We stayed up late watching movies. We went out to dinner at fancy restaurants. But when I dropped her off, I felt alone once again.

I remembered that when I was younger, how much I enjoyed dancing. Well, I thought I would return to it, and I began spending my weekends going to the city to dance.

Chapter 24: Memories of Allie

It was the heyday of lesbian dancing in New York. A British woman came over and started several clubs for lesbians, including the "World of Women," where I went that evening. Aside from occasional excursions with my friend Sarah to a few gay clubs in the village and my times at the Old Reliable, I had never been to a lesbian club. After paying to enter, I walked into a long bar that stretched from the entrance to the beginning of a new room. It was dark wood and beautifully carved. All along the bar, women sat and stared at each newcomer. I felt like a prostitute showing off to the women who were potential customers.

When I walked into the back room, everything changed. It was black, with lights gleaming all over in rapid succession. As my eyes adjusted to the light, I found that at the front of the room was a raised area upon which two women were dancing. The first looked like Betty Bop, with her hair cut short, bright lipstick, and stockings. The second woman was wild and danced without abandon in her tight, short skirt.

In the back of them was a giant screen showing lesbian porn. I had never been in a lesbian club like this before. As I got used to what I saw, I noticed a young man emerge and start dancing a few feet away.

I only watched his back as he never danced in front of me, but I was mesmerized by his moves. There were a few gay men in this club, not many, but a few, and I thought he was one of them. He was immaculate. His hair, shorn close on the sides, was long on the top and back and faded into a "V" in the back of his head. He had on a pale-yellow shirt, a pair of bright red suspenders, and dark trousers.

But what amazed me was not how picture-perfect his appearance was but how he danced. I was mesmerized by his movements. After a few minutes, he dove into the crowd; I could not see him. I returned to the women moving on stage when, low and behold, I saw the beautiful boy getting ready to dance.

He very slowly took off his clothes. He dropped his suspenders around his waist, removed his shirt, showing well-cut abdominals, and finally, he unzipped and slipped off his pants. It was only then that I realized that my dancer was female. I watched him dance in his underwear, never taking my eyes off his feet. I would go to the club almost every weekend to watch him. I stood in front and focused on what he was doing, having little concern for the other women, the porn show, or anything else. I did this for several weeks, and then, one evening, when he began to dance, I stepped forward and danced with him. In a very short time, we became friends and went to dinner.

I never bothered with any of the women at the club; I had only one fixation on him. I wanted to be just like him. I soon came to the club in beautiful shirts and spent a lot of money on men's slacks. I also wore suspenders: bright red but also other colors. Like Allie, I began to wear my hair short and cut it into a V in the back. It wasn't that I wanted Allie, although I would be lying to say I did not; I wanted to become Allie. I had emerged as a Butch.

Allie came and went in a brief season. She was a prostitute who was also spending her time getting a pilot's license. Allie flew small jets from Teterboro. She also worked in a strip club, wearing makeup and a dress and dancing for the men. Allie was looking for someone to pay for her flight to San Francisco, but I was unwilling and unable to do this for her. She was not a prostitute I wanted to buy but a Butch I wanted to be like. Finally, Allie went out to San Francisco. The last I heard was that she became the madame of a house there.

But the memory of Allie lives with me. It is present in the way I dance and in how I dress. I was no longer simply now the "lady" that my mother wanted me to be I was as well, a butch woman and knew myself as such.

In addition to the wholesale health food business at the core of Ki Foods, I began catering to the lesbian community. One of the reasons they hired me was because of how I dance. I would dress up like a well-dressed butch and dance for them, just as I had watched Alley dance at the club. At the age of 78, I am the star of the dance club and still dance almost as well as Allie.

Chapter 25: Memories of Seidy

I went all this time, nearly 14 years, without any desire for a relationship. I walked away from women who were interested in me. Partially, this was because I had too much responsibility to become involved with anyone whose presence might distract me. I belonged wholly and entirely to Ki Foods and exclusively to it when my children moved away. I was married to the company. But also, there was a hint in me that I was a psychopath, and so, did not really want or need anyone in my life who I could abuse. Not until Seidy.

When the World of Women closed and lesbian clubs were no longer fashionable in New York, I started going to a gay club in New Jersey to dance. I would go there, dance for several hours all alone, look at the moves the people were making and try to imitate them, and then go home alone.

One evening, I was there and went over to get a club soda at the bar when I noticed a gay boy crying. "What is wrong?" I said to him, and he proceeded to tell me the story of his life. He was a drag queen from Kansas. He worked for his father there, even though everyone knew he was gay. He had been married to a young girl at a very young age, but he knew he was not destined for marriage, so he divorced her and returned to his drag queen ways. He used to come to New York to participate in shows and then return to his family. His family accepted him, although they thought he was a little strange. His father loved and stood by him, even though he could not deal with his son being a drag queen.

He had come to New York, where he met a guy who was a bartender at this club and had gone to see the show. They quickly became lovers, and he went home to Kansas, packed a bag, and went to stay at his friend's home. However, as his friend figured out, he was a roaring alcoholic. This fact very quickly ended the relationship because the bartender did not drink and could not deal with his friend's taste for the bottle. He asked him to leave and told him to come and pick up his things when he was ready. He was standing there, crying, not knowing what to do, not knowing where to turn, when I ran into him. I took pity on him and told him that I had a large house with many empty rooms, as my children were grown, and you could stay with me. When you get ready to pick up your stuff, we will come and get it and set you off for Kansas. He was very grateful, and we went home that evening, and I gave him a room. When I came home from work the following day, he was prepared to provide me with a performance. He came, dressed as a woman, down the steps of my house and entertained me with his singing, which was really good. He was fun; of course, I didn't realize what an alcoholic he was. He came to work with me on Sunday and showed himself to be a good worker in the kitchen.

I was short a baker and asked him if he would like to stay with me and learn to bake muffins until I found someone else. He was overjoyed. The following Sunday, he was going to pick up his stuff, and I waited for him in the bar while he went and said whatever he had to say to his lover and to get his things. To kill the time, I played pool while I was waiting.

It was very early in the morning, and I was surprised to see anyone at the bar. But there was my old friend John and his lover, sitting there. They were too old to dance, but they loved the club and going there to meet friends. The other table was a young couple, one woman about 30 and another around 20. I should have paid more attention to them but proceeded with my game. All of a sudden, John came over to me and told me that Seidy, one of the women, but I knew not which one wanted to buy me a drink. I looked over, not sure who was Seidy, and said to him that I did not drink.

He returned, asking me if she could buy me a coke. Again, I said to him I didn't drink coke. Finally, he came over and asked me if I wanted a glass of milk, and I couldn't help laughing. At that point, I went over to meet Seidy. She was not the Anglo-looking 30-year-old but the younger woman. When she started to speak, I realized, on the basis of her accent, that she had arrived in America not too long ago. Her way of dealing with English was to use the word shit when she didn't know what else to say in English. Every other word was "shit." I spoke a modicum of Spanish, so it helped us to communicate. She had dark hair and eyes, but her skin was flawlessly white. It was the stark contrast between her obsidian hair and pure white skin that always fascinated me. I asked he where she was from, and she said Costa Rica. She said she and her sister-in-law, whose name I can't remember, were involved in a house cleaning company, and I, who had no time for anything, let alone cleaning my ten-room house, asked her to give me her card, and I said I would call her, and that was the end of that.

Travis came with his luggage, and we went home, where he proceeded once again to entertain me with his performance and, in the meantime, to cry about his lost lover, the bartender. Lots of fish in the sea, I said to him.

A few days later, I called Seidy to set up an appointment. But she was not interested in cleaning my house; she was interested in me. "Hello, how are you." "Fine," she said. "I was wondering when you could make it over to clean my house; it is quite large and needs a lot of work." She said, "I thought you were calling to ask about me." Well, well, "Of course, that too. Sorry, how are you." She answered by telling me she "loved me." I didn't know what to say. "But you don't even know my name?" "It doesn't matter. I fell in love with you the second I saw you. Will you please come and have dinner with me."? Well, I was taken aback. I had not fallen in love with her and told her so. "Have dinner with me she insisted." I agreed, but I did not love her and told her so. We would have dinner, look at the house, and arrive at an estimate of how much. I was not, I told her, madly in love with her or anyone else.

Yet, I would hear from Seidy less than twenty-four hours later. She called and told me that she lived with her brother, Francisco. He had found out she had taken his wife to a gay club and attacked her. Could I please come and pick her up because she too had nowhere to go? I told myself, another person in need of saving, and I went along with Trevor to see about getting her out of the situation. She came out with her luggage and got in the car. She had absolutely no signs of physical violence.

I took her home, and we got her settled in. I told her she could stay with me until she found a better place to live. "You are safe here, although you have to understand that I have no feelings for you. Are you clear?" She didn't say anything to me.

When she heard about Ki Foods, she told me she wanted to work there. I said I always had room for someone else, and if she wanted, she could work. In a little while, she was a full-fledged member of Ki Foods. She was a whiz in the kitchen, anticipating whatever the chefs may need. She knew, as well, how to get the food ready to be shipped. In time, she learned how to order for me. I was so impressed by her work ethic that she rapidly moved up in the company until she was second only to me.

In the meantime, Seidy and I became lovers. She was persistent. She was also living in my house. And the other element was that despite my relationship with Ulla, I had not learned how to make love to a woman. I was still caught up in Bart's rape fantasy and knew only how to suffer and endure sex with him. I knew nothing of kindness or gentleness. Seidy, very slowly and carefully, started to teach me the kindness and caring of a woman. In time, I had great sexual satisfaction with her. However, there was one problem, which was partially the result of her being younger than me, and this was the fact that I could not believe she loved me. In particular, I was a U.S. citizen and had my own money. I saw her as someone taking advantage of me, using me for her benefit.

The fact is that I was right and wrong. As I realized, Seidy did love me and clung to me out of need and satisfaction. But the fact of the matter was that I didn't know it then. When someone told me they loved me, they would betray and abandon me. That's what love means: betrayal and abandonment. In turn, I would fuel the desire in another person to leave so that I could resent them. In the end, I wanted to be alone.

I was impressed with her as a worker, and I needed her to help me with Ki Foods. She was very loyal to me in this respect. And, of course, we shared a lot of good times. We went out to dinner almost every night and to the gay clubs in New Jersey. We spent a lot of time traveling in the area: we went up and down the shores of New Jersey, to Vermont and New Hampshire, to campgrounds in New York State, and on the shores of North Carolina. We went apple picking and pumpkin picking. We went to New Orleans for the Mardi Gras and to Atlantic City, where Seidy spent a lot of money trying to get rich. I did not gamble but spent my time wandering around and then met Seidy at a restaurant where I teased her about how much money she had lost. We had beautiful times together. And, of course, not at first, but in time, I fell in love with her. But that meant the stronger she loved me, the harder I tried to push her away until I finally did.

It began with my verbal abuse of her. There is no question that it arose from a feeling of superiority. I screamed at everyone I worked or had a relationship with as it was part of my psychopathology. I was a superior person: I spoke English. I was more well-educated than her. I was older and wiser. I had money and a house. For all these reasons and others, I abused her. I was particularly harsh to her. At first, it was just my telling her what to do on the job, which was understandable. But it extended to all areas of my life until I finally called her "a bag of garbage" whenever we fought.

If I was abusive, Seidy contributed to this by her great need to provoke jealousy in me. She would look at women while I was watching her. I would, of course, get furious, and she would be contrite. However, whenever she had the opportunity, she went on to more severe forms of cheating. She began to have an affair with a woman whom she met quite casually at one of her drunken gatherings with her friend. She would wait for me to sleep, and then, hearing the snoring, she would call the woman. I found the number a short time later on my phone bill. I called and spoke to the woman's girlfriend, who told me Seidy was considering moving in together. Of course, I became outraged. I went home, changed the lock on our apartment, packed Seidy's bags, and sent them to a nearby motel.

I took her back but remembered the incident and threw her out again. I could not get over her cheating on me. It went on like this for a long time until, at last, she left me permanently. She went to live in a dark, dismal apartment in the basement of a building in West New York. I visited her, and we made love. I often asked her to return to me, but she never did.

My jealousy was developed in me by Seidy. I am, to be sure, jealous, but not intrinsically so. I trusted my partner and felt no need for jealousy, but the fact of the matter was that her provocation evoked it in me. I was abusive, but she played the game of jealousy quite well. It was at the core of her being.

As it turned out, her mother was a prostitute in San Isidro, Costa Rica. She had a crush on Frank and wound up having Seidy with him. Frank had plans to go to the capital, San Jose, and study to become a physician's assistant. Of course, he would not marry her and convinced her he would send money for the baby, so there was no need to go to court. She believed him, and off he went. In time, he did send some money and gifts for the child, but it was different from what she expected him to send. Nor was this his only child; he had eleven other children by several women. He was, after all, a physician's assistant and earned a relatively large amount of money for a Costa Rican. But Seidy was last on his list. She told me one story: seeing him in the street with another woman. She went over to say hello, and he just walked by, ignoring her. The pain was awful.

When she was younger, she lived with her grandmother, and these were some of her life's best years. But her mother, looking for a husband and finding instead a long list of men willing to sleep with her, got pregnant again and again. In time, she moved into a small cabin in the city of San Isidro and began to ply her trade.

It was tiny, with just four rooms and an outdoor kitchen where she cooked and washed. It was poorly put together, with large slats in the wood, and there in that cabin, she raised five children. She had a son named Franklin and three more sons. When she went out to find a man, she would be gone for an extended period, and during that time, Seidy took care of the younger children. She fed them, took care of the laundry, and watched over them until her mother got home, and, more often than not, she was pregnant again. To Seidy's mind, this meant that if a woman left the house, no matter for how long, she would sleep with a man and come home pregnant, and this became an obsession so that if I or anyone else left her, even to go to the grocery store, it meant that I was sleeping with a man. I told her I did not intend to sleep with anyone else and that her jealousy was unjustified. But she never stopped.

Jealousy was the game we played. Seidy was jealous of my relationship with men, and I was jealous of her lust for women, and this was the bond that held us in our messed-up relationship. In the end, she was driven to wander, and then, when she wandered, I threw her out. I threw her out, and the inside of me hurt. I took her back and then threw her out again. This was the name of the game we called jealousy.

But I have to say, for the good times we had together, for the lust we shared in bed, for all the conversations that lasted well into the night, I loved Seidy as much as I loved anyone, and I was sorry that I was abusive towards her when I should have been more understanding.

As an aside, some twenty years after my relationship with Seidy, I returned to America and found her again. I was walking into a store when I felt a hand on me. I turned around and saw Seidy. We embraced as old lovers do and told each other how much we loved one another. Time had not changed us.

Chapter 26: Memories of Lake Wekiva

I continued to work at KI Foods without Seidy. I was lost without her and felt her absence at every moment. It went on like this for almost six months before the World Trade Center bombing. I went to work early, only to discover we needed some things. I set out for the restaurant supply place in Hackensack, where I could pick up some supplies. When I came home, the newscasters told me that a small plane had flown into the World Trade Center and that smoke was coming out, but nothing more. By the time I got back to the shop and turned on my TV, the beginning of what had happened was revealed to me for a short while until the TV shut off. The World Trade Center had been attacked. I understood that there would be no delivery of food. I told my employees to stop working, piled them in a truck, and we went to a cliff on the Palisades so that we could watch. I told them they were witnessing a moment that would live in American history. And then we went back, cleaned up, and I sent them home. We showed up for work the next day, but I found out the National Guard was holding up traffic at the George Washington Bridge and checking every truck as it went into New York. The same was confirmed at the Lincoln and Holland tunnels. So, I sent them home again.

I discovered that the Trade Center had been hit by not just one plane but by two planes. Of course, by now, Ki Foods was primarily located in New York. I had accounts at the World Trade Center and around the building itself. New York had become my primary location and now that I could not go anywhere near the World Trade Center, much of my business was lost. I was also having such a difficult time getting my trucks into New York as I was shipping prepared foods. I saw my company's value sink to nothingness. I told my guys they had to find more work; there was nothing I could do now. I called up one of my colleagues who had been looking to rent my kitchen when I wasn't using it. Of course, there were only a few hours I wasn't using it when I was busy, but now it was completely free. There was no business to sell, only pieces of equipment. I told him that if he would take my plant as it was for a fixed sum, he could have the plant immediately. He took me up on it, and I found myself free at last, for what I felt was a tremendous burden taken off my shoulders and not the loss of my business. I felt, for the first time in my life, completely free.

My children were grown, I had sold my house and was now living in an apartment, and I had embarked on another relationship with a woman who I thought could help me get over Seidy. She was living in Florida, and I went down to visit her in Orlando, and she came up to visit me, for the short period of time I had to spend with her before I finished my business. She was pleasant enough, but was no great love in my life, which I felt was particularly important to me. Nor was making love to her quite as stupendous as making love to Seidy, for she lacked any desire to satisfy me. I was still in love with Seidy and would remain so for many years. Vanita, was just a distraction and I regarded her as such.

So, everything happened quite suddenly. The effects of the World Center bombing ended my business. Vanita had entered my life a month or so before. My children were living their lives on their own. I was suffering from my breakup with Seidy, and I was in deep depression because of it. When Vanita suggested I move to Florida with her, I decided to go. She flew up, and we packed up my things. I left the apartment to my daughter Brooke with most of my furniture in it, and we set off for Florida. While we were driving down, Vania congratulated herself on having "gotten the girl," and I looked at her and thought that she hadn't gotten me at all. I was just moving along, and Seidy was still on my mind.

Vanita worked nights as a nurse, which meant that she was gone most of the night. She would call me early in the morning, when she had finished working at five AM or so, wake me up, and asked me if I wanted to have breakfast with her. This was outrageous to me, and I told her so. Why would she wake me up particularly when I had to go to work to have breakfast with her? What she wanted was someone to be there when she needed them and go away when she didn't need them. I was taking the place of her mother, who would feed and nourish her and then go away when she felt the need to sleep. And she felt the need to sleep more than anyone I have ever known; it was a joy to sleep and burdensome to be awake. When she was asleep, she had beautiful dreams, and when she was awake, had to face the harsh glare of reality. Reality was that she was getting older, fatter, and less attractive, although she was an attractive woman.

While Vanita was living out her fantasies in sleep and bed, I spent my time wandering around Orland. It was, to my mind, such a beautiful place to live. It had thousands of lakes of various sizes. When I left Vanita I went and bought myself a kayak and put it in the back of my truck and went all over fishing and looking at the sights alone the river. I used to like to go Lake Wekiva and paddle along the shore. I have been to almost 40 countries: see the old-time beauty of Prague, watched the sunsets in the desserts of Egypt, seen the Valley of the Kings, but I have never seen anything as beautiful or as dangerous as Lake Wekiva.

I was attracted to both. It was surrounded on the shores by alligators sunning themselves in the hot Orlando sun, their mouths open so they could let the sunlight inside of them. They were everywhere in the water, and during mating season, they sounded like frogs coming from all sides. It was then that they were particularly dangerous. Then there were the Manatees who floated beneath the boat like some silent, foreign creature. And all along the way were turtles clinging to the fallen tree trunks who quickly slipped into the water when they heard you coming. And the fish were everywhere, jumping in the water. I went one time with Vanita's puppy and discovered there were some monkeys living nearby who ran to me and tried to get the puppy away from me and eat it.

When I got away from the tourist canoes who inevitably turned back at the first sight of the alligators, was the deep silence of the place. Aside from the turtles dropping into the water and sometimes the breeze surrounding me, there was dead silence and a time for me to be alone with my thoughts. While most people need the sound of something, the radio or TV, I loved absolute silence and the peace it gave me, and I found it paddling around Lake Wakiva. It gave me the opportunity to see nature and ponder it. I watched the birds flying high above me, for none dared wander to close to the alligators of the Wakiva. And every time I went there, I dared go further and further upstream, away from the tourists and their noise as they oohed and awed the gators.

Finally, it would take me a whole day just to ride north on the river and turn back. I picked oranges and grapefruit and brought them along to eat and set off for my day on the river. I saw snakes, cottonmouths, some of which had just been born but a few who were old and laid in the sun to warm themselves. Once I was paddling along and didn't watch the shore on my left side and hit a cotton mouth that arose out of the water, but it was not quite Spring, the water was cold, and he was laying around a stick trying to catch fish, so he made no move to strike me. He just lowered himself into the water once again. If it had been warmer, he would have struck me without hesitation, as cottonmouths do, their mouths showing the deep whiteness of their ferocious attack. They were perhaps the most dangerous when they hung from a tree and could land on you from above. I witnessed this when one dropped on one of the canoes. The owner was a seasoned Florida fisherman who didn't hesitate to throw the cotton mouth back into the water before it struck.

Every chance I got I went back to the Lake and paddled my kayak, sometimes to fish but other times just to glide, look and think. On this one trip, I went further up the river than I had ever gone before to an area that was nearly covered with growth from the jungle. I glided along, listening to the turtles jumping into the water, but hearing nothing else but the lovely silence. I watched an old copper mouth stretched along the river; a copper mouth is born more colorful and then grows dark in its old age, and this one was so dark he was almost black. And as I watched him, careful to make sure that he would not strike, I saw a strange clearing in the jungle. When I passed it, it seemed to me that I had seen something inside, something that looked like an old totem pole. Could it really be the remnants of an old totem pole left behind by the Indians? I paddled around to it and found I could just fit through the clearing in the jungle.

When I entered it, I found myself in a place that resembled a church; it was totally dark, except for shafts of light that penetrated the deep jungle. I didn't see any totem pole, but it did seem to me that I had entered someplace sacred, and I stopped just to take in the wonder of it all.

After I had looked around, I started to turn around and go out of the cave-like entrance, which let me in. I went a little bit and found myself stuck on the branches of the trees that grew in the water. I pushed off only to find myself caught on another branch, and then another and another. I was stuck and could not turn my kayak around. Of course, I was afraid to get out and go into the water to try and turn myself around because I had heard enough horror stories about alligators and didn't want to meet one personally. Nor could I go into the jungle for fear of snakes, for there were not only cotton mouths, but rattlesnakes.

I realized that I had gotten very tired from pushing my canoe, and seeing that my oranges and grapefruit were gone, I found myself very thirsty. I was, in a word, totally spent. I didn't know what to do and put my head down on the boat and said, "Well, here I am, in this lonely place where no one can find me, and it looks as though I will die here unless I gather up the courage to go the water and try to get out." I sat there for a few minutes when I got the feeling that someone was watching me. I wasn't sure if it was a snake or a gator, but I was certain that I was being watched, and ever so carefully, lifted my head up to find out what it was. There before me stood a giant bird, one I had never seen before in my travels up and down the river. It was standing so close to me that I imagined I was fantasizing, and I reached out my hand, ever so slowly, to touch it, to make sure it was really there. As I moved to touch it, it did not move away from me, and I touched its wings to make sure it was real. Only then, when I touched the bird, did I feel my kayak move suddenly, and in one fell swoop, I was free from the roots. The bird, which was quite large, white with some coral color on its sides, moved backwards and in three strides disappeared into the jungle. And I was free again to paddle out of my holy sanctuary and back onto the river.

I spent a lot of time searching the birds of Florida, trying to find that bird, but I never did. Then, when I had moved up North, a friend of mind sent me an article. It was about a bird that Floridians thought had gone extinct, and I cannot remember its name. And then, one day, a bunch of Florida fishermen saw this bird rise up from the water and watched it fly away, knowing it was still alive. It was that bird that came to help me in my time of want; that was the miracle that saved my life.

After I moved out of Vanita's, which took less than three months from the time I moved in, I found some work as a chef in a gourmet restaurant called "Three Fat Chefs". The owner was from Iceland, and he had studied at the Cordon Blue, and had all kinds of awards for winning Chef's competitions hung on the wall of his restaurant. I can't remember his name, but from him I learned Cordon Blue cooking, and worked for him until his restaurant closed. He surrounded himself with his friends, but each of them, in his own way, took what he wanted from the place and ran it into the ground. His partner dealt cocaine in the storage room in back; his maître de took advantage of his collection of fine wines; his head chef helped himself to the filet mignon's, all while the owner chased women and spent very little time at the restaurant.

Afterwards, a friend of mine suggested I go to work for Sprint. She told me they paid a good sum of money, and she was working her way through college. I went over, and they hired me, and I was sent to work at one of their less lucrative places called Costco. It was a place where no one wanted to work because you did get a good salary, but there was not enough money from commissions, and everybody wanted commissions because that was where the money was. I went to work at Costco, and quickly found out, that it was in fact a wonderful place to sell phones, because they had an unconditional return policy.

I would greet people when they came through the door and ask them if they wanted to buy a phone. This was in the early days of cell phones, when they really didn't have a lot of coverage, and so most people didn't really want to buy one. I showed them what a cell phone could do, and then I told them about the unconditional return policy at Costco, the one that allowed them to bring the phone back and get their money. I sold so many phones because of this, that I broke all records. I was the start salesman for cell phones in the Orlando area, and enjoyed my work, talking to people about their lives. This went on for quite a while until they stopped their "boots on the ground" attempt to sell their phones, which were, by that time, selling very well on their own.

Once I left Vanita's and moved into my own apartment, I found that living in Orlando was quite enjoyable. I was fishing, going kayaking along the Wakiva and other lakes, and riding my bicycle in my spare time. In addition, I was also returning to my life before Ki Foods, to my life as a scholar. This was very difficult after 15 years of no intellectual stimulation. Vanita always made fun of me because I was an "intellectual" while she was more mystical, sitting around and meditating in front of her Guru. But I was not intellectual, I had dropped it all behind me when I started Ki Foods and now had to return to it. I began to read books from the library and eventually returned to my way of life.

I didn't have any profession which I could pursue when I ran into one of my colleagues from Sprint. She told me that a local school named The Stenographic Institute was looking for teachers. I went over there, showed them my academic credentials, and was hired on the spot.

I taught Medical Terminology, which I had picked up as a medical secretary many years ago, and Law, which I was vaguely familiar with. I had returned to teaching, such as it was, and I was happy. Teaching anything was better than not teaching at all. But then, my family called me. Tiel was having problems with her husband as well as problems with her daughter TJ. She asked me to come home, and help her out, and I went home once again.

Chapter 27: Memories of Coming Home

I made my way north, passing alligator roadkill in Florida, the Palmetto Bugs in Carolina, past Washington, D.C., and onward to the New Jersey Turnpike and home to my family.

Tiel and Emile had played together since birth. Even when I moved to Staten Island, Marianthe regularly visited me alone with her son. Then, out of fear that Henry and his new wife would take Emile away from her, she moved to Canada, and over time, I lost touch with her. I was trying to get a new account in the West Village when someone behind me asked if there was any place to get vitamins. I turned around and there was Marianthe. She lives in New York now with her husband, Adolph. I was happy to see her and invited her, her husband, and Emile to my house for Thanksgiving Dinner, which was happening next week. I asked Marilyn, Larry, and Kevin, as well, and we spent a lot of time reminiscing about the Lower East Side, the Old Reliable, and the children when they were little. Kevin was 21, Emile was behind him at 21, and Tiel was 20.

After dinner, Larry and Adolph searched for a TV to watch football; Marilyn, Marianthe, and I went to the kitchen table for our coffee, and Tiel and Emile began cleaning the table.

As we were enjoying our coffee, we looked up at Tiel and Emiel and saw them staring at each other in rapt attention, their eyes never leaving the other's body. When they left, Marilyn said, "Did you see that?" "Yep," I said. "Wouldn't it be incredible if they married?" said Marilyn. They had played with each other since they were tiny babies, and I had pictures of them when they were toddlers. "Oh," said Marianthe, "she wouldn't marry him as he is such a jerk."

It was the story I told at their wedding. Henry was there soaking up the spotlight with his second wife, Camille. Marianthe and Adolf were there, along with Marilyn and Larry. Sometime later, Tiel and Emile had a son, Emile Jr., I took a picture of Henry, Emile, and Emile Jr. and thought that my past and present all came together in that moment; Henry, Marianthe, Jose, and I had the same grandchild.

Now, Tiel and Emile were living in Union City, New Jersey, in a house they had just bought. It was still primarily a Cuban neighborhood but included Guatemalan, Peruvian, Colombian, Salvadorans, and Costa Ricans. It was a Hodge podge of Latin Cuisine that stretched through Hudson County and encompassed every neighborhood until you hit the Turkish/Armenian section of Cliffside Park, where it ended in a bevy of excellent Armenian restaurants.

It was not that they lived in a Latino community that bothered me, as I was very familiar with Latino communities; it was the fact that the house Tiel lived in was old and looked more like a tenement. The rooms were railroad, meaning they were one on top of the other from front to back. In this respect, it was very much like my grandmother's place or, for that matter, the tenements on the Lower East Side. No windows were in the remaining rooms, just one in the front and one in the back. Moreover, to my mind, it was in one of the ugliest sections of an ugly city. The Lincoln Tunnel emptied into it, and it was simply a haven of bad air.

Moreover, the buildings on either side of it were close together, with some having no walkways between them. There were, to be sure, beautiful buildings: old houses that dated back to the German and Swiss who owned the embroidery centers for which the community was famous. There were also beautiful mansions along the Hudson River that looked out over New York, but the wealthy upper classes owned these and not the workers who labored for them. The rest was a hodge-podge of buildings built on top of one another. It remains today one of the most populated areas of the country, and it was and is a poor and oppressed area. However, it has become gentrified as people begin to move into it, looking for a place to live away from Manhattan's expensive apartments.

I could not believe my Tiel and her husband bought this place to live in. It took me only a short time to convince Tiel that her railroad apartment did not suit her and get her to look for a new place. Emile, on the other hand, was extraordinarily cheap. He had grown up poor and saved every penny he could, even when he didn't have to. The place appealed to him because it had a second apartment below, and the five children and their parents paid his rent for him. The fact that this was quite dangerous and occasionally gave way to fires didn't matter. Neither did the eldest son's alcoholism. All that mattered was saving money, which he poured into his retirement fund. He and Tiel worked on Broadway in union jobs: Tiel was working on costumes; she attended the Fashion Institute of Technology at a time when they were taking 1 out of 100 students. On black and red velvet, Tiel designed a replica of a Chinese kite, hand-stitched and filled with beautiful colors, so she was accepted. I was proud of her because she was an artist, as I had been in my younger years.

Emile was moving furniture in and out of the theaters. They could easily afford something better. Still, he worked extraordinary hours with tons of overtime, and so the conditions under which he and his family, now including a boy named Emile, Jr., were unimportant to him. He was doing what he was supposed to: working all the time and saving money. He once had a massive fight with Tiel because she had spent an extra dollar on the cell phone bill.

On the other hand, Tiel had lived with Bart and me and so had grown accustomed to having what she wanted whenever she wanted it. They were at polar extremes regarding money, one of their problems. It turned out to be huge because Tiel was bipolar, although no one knew it at the time, and her partner was a frugal freak.

We went to look for a house. As it turned out, the price of homes had increased, both in Union City and the country. Emile didn't want to move, and Tiel wasn't sure what she wanted except to get out of her ghetto apartment. Emile was at work when Tiel got a call to look for a house in West Orange, New Jersey. When we got there, I was so impressed. It was a huge home, thirteen rooms in all. But most of all, it was on a double lot and was graced with a beautiful garden: cedar and oak trees surrounded a secluded area that allowed for complete privacy. It was also on one of the prestige avenues in West Orange, the lone line of homes that got increasingly more expensive as you went down Gregory Avenue. Ours was at the very beginning, but we had, as the saying goes, "arrived." Without ever seeing the house, I told the woman that we would pay double the asking price if they lowered the house by ten thousand. She accepted, and early the following day, Tiel got a call and was told that the house was hers.

As it turned out, we made enough money from her tenement house to buy this one and still have leftover money. Emile now had a house he lived in for free and money to put towards his growing retirement fund. He loved to talk about money and how much he saved; it was his only and primary obsession. Tiel, on the other hand, could not wait to spend it.

I moved in with Tiel, trying to play the role of a devoted mother. She was my oldest daughter, my pride and joy. But I had no idea of what she really was, although it all fell into place for me when I lived with her when she was an adult.

Chapter 28: Memories of Moving On

When I first found out I was pregnant, I went to see a famous fortune teller on the Lower East Side to find out the sex of my child and the kind of personality it would have. The older man told me that I would have a girl and that she would expect the very best in life. "What do you mean I asked." "She will be a woman who will not settle for mink but will demand ermine." His prophecy turned out to be true.

Tiel behaved like a princess, and everyone treated her as a princess. It was because she was so beautiful. Both Jose and I treated her as such, and my husband Bart catered to her needs, and so did her sisters. As she grew older, her husband, cheap though he was, still tried to make her happy, particularly after she was diagnosed with Bipolar disease. She sent him a birthday greeting that said, "All good things in life came from him." It was true; he worked so hard to see that she had what she wanted, or at least most of the time. But when she had her daughter, TJ was not the princess of her life but rather the servant who waited on the princess. TJ did everything she could to make her Moher happy: cleaned, helped around the house, and watched her brother. In turn, she received little gratitude for her efforts but heard constant complaints about what she had done wrong in trying to do right. What was true of TJ was also true of me. When I went to live with her, Tiel and Emile went to a wedding in Vermont. TJ and I spent the entire weekend cleaning the house to surprise Tiel. Tiel didn't even notice but saw one minor thing: the sponge was in the sink and not put where it belonged and for this, she chastises us. That was all she had to say about our efforts.

When I went to live with Tiel, I tried my best to be a good grandmother: I helped the kids with their homework, cooked dinner, did the dishes, took the little boy to swimming lessons, and did the laundry. I did everything I could to make her life easier. One day, she said she wanted to talk to me. She was sitting in a leather armchair, her computer in her hands, and told me we had to get things straightened out. First of all, when I did the laundry, I did not put the clothes away fast enough, and so the cats were sitting on it. I used to leave dinner for them as they came in late. On this particular night, I made meatloaf. She told me this was unacceptable. And what kind of gravy did I put on it? Didn't I know they were trying to lose weight? And I had to spend more time with TJ on her homework. And I should pay for half of the lessons for my Grandson because I was going into the pool while he was learning how to swim. I looked at her, turned around, showed her my butt, and told her to please kiss it. Then, I went upstairs, packed my bags, and left. It was TJ I felt sorry for, and I told her so, but I could not stand being criticized. She said it would be worse if I left, and I said "TJ, I can't stay." In reality, this was a selfish mistake. Tiel drove TJ to the brink of insanity before she went insane herself.

TJ was a good-natured child who grew frustrated by her mother's constant criticisms. In her later years, Tiel diagnosed her as bipolar and engaged in this long process of having TJ analyzed. But the fact was that it was not TJ who suffered from bipolar disease, but Tiel. It wasn't until she was in her late 40's that Tiel was diagnosed. By then, the damage to TJ had been done, and she got pregnant, at the age of 16, by a young man and moved in with him. She was way too young; he was a loser and a half. He beat her and did drugs, and eventually, she left him. She is now living in Ireland with her two children. But she suffered miserably because of her mother. When Tiel finally got diagnosed, it was TJ who took her to the mental institution where she stayed. Emile stepped in and took over the family, and after a while, Tiel returned home. But she was still the princess, now more than ever. Her bipolarity ensured it.

Brooke was leaving my apartment to live with her boyfriend, and I moved in just in time. I got a job at Hudson County Community College, teaching English Composition. It was beautiful to be a professor again, if for no other reason than it satisfied my psychopathic need for approval. To teach English Composition, I also had to teach English as a Second Language. I had to do this to get the job, so I taught one class in addition to teaching English Composition. In time, my career was developing, and I was teaching Rhetoric, and Critical Thinking., which is what I called Dialectics. I thought about moving on to another, finer institution after a couple of tears.

Two things stopped me. One was a student I had in my English Composition Class. Her writing could have been better. It made no sense. I offered to teach her independently, as I always did, but she had no interest. After a few more essays, I thought she did not want to take classes with me and offered counseling at the writing center. She took advantage of both of these and continued to get good grades. She asked me once why she got terrible grades and the other students did not. I said that she made no effort to improve, which was why. She was quiet after that, and her essays did not improve.

I was called to speak to the Dean of Arts and Sciences a few weeks later. He told me that the young woman had gotten a lawyer and threatened to sue the university because she was discriminated against. I was told in so many words that I had to pass her. I refused. At the end of the year, and despite her flunking the examination, she was given a pass for the year. I was thoroughly disgusted.

Then, I received an email from a company saying, "Congratulations, you have been hired to teach English in Russia". I thought it was a joke and looked up the company, English First, to see if it was legitimate. Yes it was. I wasn't sure what to do, so I asked my friend Suzanne what she thought. She was making dinner for her husband and didn't even turn around to talk to me. "How old are you?" she asked. "I'm 62, I said." "Well, how many adventures do you have left in life?" With that, I accepted the offer. I took a leave of absence from the university, packed my things, and told the landlord that I would be back in about six months and looking for a new apartment, and off

I went to Moscow. I fully expected to come back in time for the next semester. I would not return home for sixteen years.

Chapter 29: Memories of Moscow Nights

As I was preparing to leave America for Russia, the old Soviet song "Moscow Nights" danced through my mind and made me yearn for the Moscow of my dreams.

"All is standing still till sunrise.
If you only knew, how dear are you
Magic Moscow nights.
If you only knew, how dear are you
Magic Moscow nights.
River moving on and not moving on,
All in moon light.
You can hear the song and not hear the song
On those quiet Moscow nights.
https://lyricstranslate.com[1]

The words haunted my mind when I arrived at the airport. I was greeted by a small woman whose name I can't remember. She spoke English very well. We picked up the luggage, two cumbersome suitcases, and struggled to put them in the car. My navy-blue blazer and white slacks were filthy from the effort. The ride back to Moscow went through extensive forests of birch trees, which was amazing because we do not have many birches in America. As we approached Moscow, the pollution fell upon us, and soon, we were driving through a dark grey and yellow cloud that enveloped us. It was not the Moscow I had dreamed of for so long.

We arrived at our destination, on the outskirts of Moscow, in a town called Zhulebino. It did not look much like Moscow either. It was filled with twenty-storied, primarily new buildings stacked one on the

---

1.   https://lyricstranslate.com/

en/%D0%BF%D0%BE%D0%B4%D0%BC%D0%BE%D1%81%D0%BA%D0%BE%D0%B2

%D0%BD%D1%8B%D0%B5-%D0%B2%D0%B5%D1%87%D0%B5%D1%80%D0%B0-mos

cow-nights.html

other. We went into one of the older buildings, and when we arrived, my first impulse was to get on a plane and go back home. It was worse than the worst tenement I had lived in on the Lower East Side. A large metal door opened into a legion of garbage, filling the air with its scent. There was graffiti in the foyer, the mailboxes were falling off their frames, and the floor was filthy.

I turned around and told the woman I could not live there. She just continued to walk on. We went into the elevator, covered with graffiti, not having been washed since Soviet times, and made our way up to my floor. We passed through one door, which was the door to the apartments, then through another door, which was the door to my side of the apartments, and finally through the door to my apartment. When I opened the door, I was shocked. There were two rooms: a large room on the left, a kitchen in front of me, and a smaller foyer. All of these were covered with bits and pieces of different wall covering.

The apartment was a throwback to Soviet times. In the front room, a carpet graced the wall as it did in ancient Soviet apartments, a symbol of status and prestige. Under it, an old mattress stood. I don't know what it was made of, but it reminded me of straw. I never slept there. On the opposite side was an old Soviet storage unit with book shelving and drawers. Next to this was the window side of the apartment, which opened into a small area for drying clothes. Mine was used as a storage area for old furniture. Then, against the last wall was an old couch circa 1950's. An overhead lamp, broken on one side, hung from the middle of the room.

In the kitchen, which was very tiny, were the refrigerator, a stove, a table, and a small chair on which you could sit but which had no backing. The kitchen had a sink so tiny you could only wash a dish or two in it. I opened the kitchen cabinet and found one fork, knife, and two spoons for soup and tea or coffee.

The bathroom was pure Soviet, with one handle for the sink, which could be swung over to fill the tub. However, there was a small washing machine for laundry as no laundromats existed in the Soviet Union. I always said Stalin had laid the floor because it was old, filled with discoloration and dents. Welcome to the real U.S.S.R. I thought.

I met the Head of the School only to discover that I would teach not adults or teenagers but seven to ten-year-olds. I told them I could no longer live in my apartment or teach here, but what would I do? I would get the money back for my flight, but only after I had finished my contract. Another teacher from England hired to teach there told me that I could get a job in the company's corporate division teaching English as a Second Language to adults in various corporations. I stopped by to see them, and they hired me on the spot. I told them they had to get me a newer apartment in another section of town, one closer to the city. They did this immediately, and I found a renovated apartment with Spanish tiled floors, a built-in kitchen, and new furniture. I moved out of my place over the weekend. My new apartment in Perovo was just a few Metro stops from the city's center. Now, I walk not through modern and ancient high-rise apartments built one after the other in Zuhlebino, but old Moscow streets filled with beautiful pastel-colored buildings. In the evening, I went out for dinner at a multitude of restaurants. At night, I sometimes walked by the Moscow River and thought of my song:

River moving on and not moving on,

All in moon silver light.

This was the Moscow I dreamed of and eventually grew to love.

It was the heyday of "Puntin's Moscow." The Oligarchs, the "new capitalists of Russia," had been brought into place by Putin. They may have chosen him, but he was not about to submit to them. He gathered them together and told them that everything they had stolen so far was theirs but that this was the beginning of the end for them. He was in charge of Russia, and it was not that money equated to power but that access to power determined who had money.

He turned himself next to the oil industry. Until then, the oil barons worldwide took advantage of Russia, splitting the profits for themselves and leaving a small portion for Russia. Now, he put them in their place. Russia would receive the bulk of the oil sales, and the capitalists would receive the minority and pay for exploration.

He turned himself onto society as a whole. Plenty of gang-related activities were going on, mainly carried out by hoodlums. They would be brought into check. There would be one gang that ruled Russia, which was Putin's. Beer and vodka, which were sold on every street corner and which people would buy before they went on the Metro and the buses, were eliminated. People were not allowed to drink anywhere and everywhere, and doing so was a crime, as were so many "acceptable" things.

The old Soviet atheism, which dominated the masses, was soon transformed into the rule of the Church. So was the status of women, who were, ideally, destined to bring forth new babies every year. The power of males, which was always a part of Russian society, became more formalized; the man was the head of the household, and everyone bowed to him. At the insistence of the Church and with Putin's approval, it was no longer illegal for a man to beat his wife. Everything, from the economy to the oil industry, through Russian society and the power of the Church, was now how Putin wanted it to be. A man was a man, and a woman was a woman, and there was no room for homosexuality in this equation. He was satisfied with his country and claimed it held to traditional values, which are very much like "traditional values" all over the world, male dominance over women and hostility to homosexuality; within this context, men, real men, were proud and masculine "defenders" of the fatherland.

And the economy thrived, and the people submitted to his power; Putin was leading Russia to greatness. Walking through the streets, I saw BMWs and Mercedes everywhere I went. It was the time to be in Russia as an English teacher. I stopped working for English First and went alone to teach English. As more and more people became wealthy, they dreamed their children should learn English. My life went from one child to the other and from one adult to the other as I made more and more money. My American friend, Craig, and I teased each other: "How much money did you make?" He used to make the most, one hundred and fifty dollars an hour when the ruble traded at twenty-five rubles to the dollar. Life was good.

Chapter 30: Memories of Times Past

Russia has a lenient policy on vacations, which heralded back to the Soviet Union, so I had the opportunity to travel a lot. I went to Cyprus and then to Prague. Never having been destroyed by the Nazis, Prague was an old-time masterpiece, and I wandered through it looking at the Old Jewish areas and the Jewish cemetery. I went to Jordan and saw the wonders of Petra. I traveled down the Nile and visited ancient sites like Karnack and Luxor. On another trip to Sharm El Sheik, I went snorkeling. I knew then that God did not merely part the sea; he also had to make the mountains below the sea straight for the Jews to pass through.

I went on numerous occasions to Vilnius, the land of my Mongol ancestors, for Vilnius, like Lida, Belarus, was given to us by Vytautas the Great, king of the Polish-Lithuanian empire, for our bravery and courage in the battle of Grunwald. I visited some Boltuc relatives, my grandmother's brother's grandsons, in Bialystok, Poland. I went to London many times: once to visit the British Museum and once to visit the Belarusian Museum, where I researched my family, the Boltucs, and Yackshinas (Jacsina). On another trip, I spent time at the Marx Memorial Museum, where Lenin wrote Iskra. I had already visited Scotland when I was in America and now went on to Wales. I met with an old friend from America in Paris, and we made love as if inspired. I went on several trips to Kyiv before the war. I went to Georgia and visited Stalin's home and the Stalin Museum. Montenegro was gorgeous. I went to Bulgaria to see the oldest golden jewelry in the world. I traveled to Albania, Bosnia, and Herzegovina. It had long been a dream of mine to visit Greece, and I went there and saw the Parthenon and the Agora, where Socrates walked, and took a trip to the Oracle at Delphi. It was utterly enthralling. I went to Pattaya and was overwhelmed by the number of elderly males chasing after young girls. In the hotel I stayed at, which was quite lovely, I was next door to an older man who had a young girl brought to him every night. I visited Cambodia, where I rode elephants and walked the magic of Angkor Wat. I took a train from Estonia to Latvia, stopping at the old cities of Riga and Tallinn.

In Romania, I visited Bran Castle, the home of Dracula. I had been to Italy with Ulla when I was still in America and did not want to go back. But this time, I went to the island of Syracuse, where Archimedes cried, "Eureka." I saw the Roman ruins and had wonderful dinners at Ortigia, the island off the coast of Syracuse. At the Ear of Dionysius, I heard the murmurings of other visitors far away from me. I spent hours at the beach and evenings in town listening to Jazz. Syracuse was, without question, one of my favorite vacations. Azerbaijan was my worst. After one leaves the city of Baku, with its beautiful restaurants, there is nothing left to see but endless oil wells. Then, there was Turkey. I went there twice. Once, I went to Istanbul, where I visited the Mosques, ran through the spice market repeatedly, took a trip up the Bosporus, and bought endless scarves from street vendors. I went there again with Olga to the Turkish Riviera, where we lay on the rugged stony shore during the day, and at night, we laid on soft sheets and learned the magic of our bodies.

Sixteen years of my life passed as I went from one student to another, from one country to another, in endless progression. I loved living this way, belonging to no one, and in constant movement.

Chapter 31: Memories of The Margarita Rudomino All State Library for Foreign Literature

I was having dinner with a friend leaving for America to get his M.A. in education. During the conversation, he asked me if I could fill in as a volunteer at the Margarita Rudomino All Russian State Library for Foreign Literature. He was leaving, and they had yet to find a volunteer. I didn't want to, as I wouldn't say I liked teaching for free, but I agreed. I went over and was told that all I had to do every week was teach random students for a quarter of an hour each for one hour. That was it. The library had a French, Spanish, and German section, along with the American Center. It was run by an old group of Soviet citizens who had been there most of their lives, and it was filled with a variety of Americans who introduced the students to American culture, whether deliberately or not. There was a course in dancing, American slang, music, and business; whatever the Americans wanted, they could come there and teach a lesson. Of course, most Americans did not have an advanced degree, but it didn't matter. They had a wonderful time with the Russian students, who, in turn, became familiar with the American language and culture.

I had been teaching there for almost a year when the old Soviets were dismissed, and a new group of three new managers were hired. The first thing they did was fire the entire American group because they were not "qualified." These were clearly "Putin's people," if not Putin's, someone close to Putin. They wanted to stop unqualified Americans from teaching about American culture and replace them with Russian academics who could only lecture in Russian. Thus, The American Center would be turned into a Russian center in which courses, such as American Literature, were taught in Russian and not English. They did not let me go, however, as I was well qualified.

Since Halloween was coming, they called me in and asked me to teach a class on some monster appropriate to the occasion. I offered them Frankenstein, and they accepted. It was their way of watching me to see if I fit into their plans.

I arrived at my class and found the three new managers and ten students, which were all allowed. I began by telling them I had three things in common with Mary Wollstonecraft Godwin Shelly, the author of Frankenstein. We shared the same name, Mary, had the same birthday, August 1, and were feminists. I then told them something about the Romantics. The movement of people away from the countryside and farmland and into the cities was the driving force of the Industrial Revolution. Romanticism was a reaction against this and a desire to return to nature.

Then, I told them about Frankenstein. In 1816, Mary, Percy, and Lord Byron competed to see who could write the best ghost story. The idea for her novel came to Mary in a dream. "I saw the pale student of unhallowed art kneeling beside the thing he had put together. I saw the hideous phantasm of a man stretched out and then, on the working of some powerful engine, show signs of life and stir with an uneasy, half-vital motion. Frightful must it be, for supremely frightful would be the effect of any human endeavor to mock the stupendous mechanism of the Creator of the world. His success would terrify the artist; he would rush away from his odious handiwork horror-stricken." Frankenstein and his Monster were born together, and when he sees what he has done, Victor Frankenstein cuts himself off from his creation, but it is too late.

Then, we begin to trace how the Monster becomes more human and how Frankenstein refuses to do anything to appease the Monster and, in the process, becomes more monstrous. The Monster, driven by the need to live, finds a poor family of villagers. Living with them, he discovers he's like them in mind but not flesh and is finally driven away when people realize he is a monster. "I admired virtue and good feelings and amiable qualities of my cottagers, but I was shut out from intercourse with them, except through means which I obtained by stealth when I was unseen and unknown, and which rather increased than satisfied the desire I had of becoming one among my fellows."

He returns once again to Victor to make him a wife. "I'm alone and miserable, man will not associate with me but as deformed and horrible as myself." He tells Victor to make him a companion "of the same species and have the same defects." Victor tries to create a wife for the Monster but finally stops the process. He cannot make two monsters. Now, the Monster will exact vengeance on Victor, ensuring he loses what is precious to him: his family.

After I told the story, we began discussing who the Monster was: Victor Frankenstein or the creature he created. Afterward, I looked at the managers and students and saw how impressed they were. I was what I had always been: a great teacher and lecturer. My narcissistic ego was satisfied. The managers asked me what other courses I could teach, and I offered them critical thinking. They accepted, not knowing what critical thinking was or how dangerous it was to teach it to students.

Three students were so impressed with the lecture that they signed up for my class. First, there was Sergei Brekhlov, who proved to me how loyal Moscow friends could be. There was Gregory, who came to every class and tried to master critical thought. He has been my friend up until the present. Finally, there was Olga, who paid little attention to my teachings but would become the great love of my life.

Chapter 32: Memories of Critical Thinking

What is Critical Thinking? I ask my students and receive various replies: it is analytical thinking, it involves taking things apart to understand them, it is innovative thinking, etc. It is none of these things, I reply. Critical thinking generally means almost exactly what it means in daily usage. You look at what something is, such as the fact that someone is fat, and criticize them for not being thinner. Put more precisely, what something is determines what it could, should, or ought to be. Then there is the question of how he got to be obese, which involves the individual's history and his family's eating habits, for example. Even more broadly, it includes the eating habits of his nation: Americans are obese people, which is a significant factor in determining why many individuals are overweight. The extensive use of sugar and corn syrup in American foods is partly responsible. On the other hand, the person could have a physiological problem that caused his obesity, such as hypothyroidism, and we would have to consider this factor in making our decision.

As we pause to examine why a person is obese, we also have to consider all the things that have not affected him. He ignores his weight, and this means that he does not belong to the small minority of the population who do watch their weight and exercise. He can be part of the American population or be a member of an impoverished country that does not have enough money for food.

From the dimension of time, we find he is one of the few humans with the luxury of being overweight. For much of humanity, the struggle for survival has meant that most people have been thin, always looking for more to eat. Many have died from hunger because they could not get enough to eat. The tendency to put on more weight than is desired is a contemporary problem.

In this way, I taught my students to look at various ways, in time and space, to think critically about something. One of the things I used to do was bring my cast iron frying pan and ask them to think critically about it. I told them I had gotten the frying pan from my first husband, who had gotten it from his mother. After some conjecture, we arrived at the fact that she had gotten in from a store. We drew a picture of my husband, his mother, and then the store. Who was responsible for bringing it to the store: well, the driver was responsible, as was the truck? Who were the workers who had made the truck? We put them on the blackboard alone with the driver. At the store, we had to count the person who unpacked it, put it on the shelves, and sold it to us. Then there was the wrapping it was put into: who was responsible for it? We counted more people. Where did the iron come from: from the foundry? Here, we add more people involved in the making of my frying pan. Then, the workers in the mine: more people were added to our original drawing.

Then I asked them the critical question: where did the iron in the mines come from? Well, iron is originally made from the fusion of elements in stars. The iron found on earth comes from meteorites, a large stellar explosion called a supernova after the lifetime of a star is exhausted.

The Earth's iron was formed when the first organism capable of photosynthesis began releasing oxygen into the oceans, which combined with dissolved iron to produce hematite or magnetite. But iron came to us from the stars. As I tell my students when I make breakfast in my frying pan, I leach iron into what I am making, and in my body, it converts into iron which feeds my blood. Carl Sagan once said, "We are made from star stuff."

My class was very popular, mainly because Russian education was based on rote learning. Students memorize what they are told and then vomit it back to the teacher. The teacher grades them on their ability to retain as much as possible. I used to call this the "The Sponge Bob

School of Rote Learning." Critical thinking taught them how to think of things in an evolutionary and internally related way.

Chapter 33: Memories of The Unity of Opposites

I had a therapist who told me that we had invisible antennas that came out of our heads. We were drawn to someone when we met someone whose antennas matched ours. Olga's antenna was an absolute match for mine. She was not the opposite of me; she was the polar opposite. Olga was not just different; she was my difference. I was a psychopath who was mean, cruel, egotistical, aggressive, who cared only about myself. Olga was a kind, gentle, self-effacing, nonaggressive person who seemed to care more about others than themselves. Our antennas matched perfectly. Or so it seemed.

Unlike other people, whose self-meanderings used to annoy me, nothing she said was unimportant to me, nor was she someone I used when needed and dismissed when I did not. Instead, I found everything Olga did and said was significant to me. I was interested in every aspect of her childhood, in every minute detail of her adult life. Although I did not think it then, we were two people drawn together so we could, each in the consciousness of the other, find out who and what we were. I am unsure if she achieved this, but my self-realization entirely revolved around Olga and changed me. If I didn't have Olga, I would never be aware of my psychopathic tendencies.

Olga was very aware of how words could impact people, so she was careful not to say things that would offend anyone. She was equally sensitive to how the words of others could hurt her and was forever crying because of what her husband said to her, which demeaned her. As for me, if my words hurt anyone, I was proud of myself, for I was quick and fast with my tongue and had always been so. I told the truth as I saw it and damn the consequences.

Because she wanted to avoid the looks of others who might judge her, she avoided quarrels and confrontations because any aggressive behavior was taboo to her. She was, as she liked to say, not fond of fighting for what she wanted. I, on the other hand, was shaped by my ancestors and Grandmother, who loved, above all else, to fight. I enjoyed it as she did because winning, no matter how, gave me a sense of fulfillment. As I said earlier, for many years, my heroes were the great boxers of the day, Muhammed Ali, Sugar Ray Leonard, and Roberto Duran. I always trained as a boxer, imagining myself in a ring, fighting and winning.

Olga was also particularly drawn to my confidence and charisma as a teacher; this was the world I dominated more than any other. I was narcissistic, dominant, superior to others, and, at worst, even a little sadistic to students who disagreed with me. She saw me as unique to her because I was not submissive or needy, and thus, I was not like her. I did not need protection; I was able to protect myself. Although Olga did not permit aggression in herself, she did admire those who did.

Olga was always willing to help, to sacrifice herself for the well-being of others. I remember one of the first times she came to my apartment as a lover. I stopped to cook food, and Olga went into the bathroom while I was busy in the kitchen. She had come prepared to wash the enclosure for my bathroom. Olga spent hours every day scrubbing them until they were clean. Then she started on my floor. Her desire to clean my house and do anything that helped me touched and amused me. It wasn't until much later that I saw this as a way of winning approval and much later that I saw it as a hallmark of her personality.

The need to be self-sacrificing was always in her. Olga's life was built around sacrificing her needs and wants for those of her parents, friends, lovers, and employers. She held onto people by serving them. I remember one occasion she and her mother were supposed to go somewhere with her father. Her mother told her father that either she or Olga would go, but not both of them. This was an attempt to show her dominance over the situations; her mother would show who was essential to the father, her, or Olga. In response, Olga voluntarily went home. She understood this as an act of self-sacrifice in which she gave way to her mother's ego and was sad when she thought about it.

On another occasion, she told me of her neighbors upstairs who threw their urine and feces down on the ground next to their basement apartment. Olga would run to clean these up. She loved this job primarily because no one else wanted it. It made her feel wanted, needed, and loved for what she could do for the family.

Much later, I understood that Olga controlled the truth to have people believe she was what they wanted her to be. Olga told me how she ran by an orphanage when she went to school and was so grateful because she was not there. If she was not obedient, if she did not make herself subservient, did not run to get her parents beer early in the morning, did not come home late from her friends or school, if Olga did not clean the house, in a word, do everything that was expected of her, the results were that she would wind up in an orphanage. She might have been brutalized and abused in her home, but Olga belonged there. In an orphanage, she belongs to no one and would be doomed to have no one take care of and protect her.

As a result, she learned to lie; it was second nature to her. If I wanted to tell the "truth" without fear of the consequences, Olga wanted to spare herself and others the truth because the truth seemed dangerous to her. On the one hand, it made her less likely to be liked, which was what she wanted. When directed at her, it made her cry because what Olga was revealed to her. Her husband, Michael, said things that were true but which she didn't want to hear. As a result, Olga's whole world was threatened by this, and she would cry.

Her philosophy was that if you told the person a lie to justify your behavior, they would never know if what you told them was true. She said to me after every lie, "You will never know whether I am lying or not." When she said this to me, I knew she was lying.

And so, we were perfect opposites; our antennas met. But our relationship was more than just this. I, who had never really been loved, found out what it was like. Olga, who was so self-sacrificing, hesitated before saying nasty things, clung to me in the depths of my cruelty, and showed me a degree of love I had never known. With my attention, my focus only on her and what she was doing and thinking in life, I made her understand that she had many good qualities, not the least of which was the ability to handle people. I led her to believe that she could do anything. And so, even though I loved telling the truth to the point of cruelty, and she lied to keep herself hidden, I loved her, and she loved me, or so it seemed. But that, too, could have been another lie.

Chapter 34: Memories of the Very Beginning

I had not been involved with anyone, with one exception, for nearly twenty years of my life. I had the opportunity but did not. Partially, this was the result of the attitude towards homosexuals in Russia. But it was also the result of the fact that I was only happy when I was alone. After all, wasn't that what the fortune teller had told my grandmother, that I would be alone? But when I met Olga, we were so attracted to one another that nothing else mattered. I wanted her and only her, and I loved her, now being sure what that meant.

She was one of the first people to join my Critical Thinking class, coming out of my lecture on Frankenstein. I, of course, did not recognize her. A month later, she came up behind me in the street and handed me a note saying she couldn't come to class because she had problems with her children. I was never interested in being anyone's "friend" unless there was something to gain from them. Nor was Olga a part of my inner circle of students who made up my class, those people who cared about what I was saying. She could have left at any moment, and I wouldn't care. She, however, wanted me to care about her, to be drawn to her, and so, for that reason, she had given me the note.

One day, after class, I went to see the people at the library as I was having trouble with my cell phone. I received huge bills and needed to learn how to deal with the phone company as I didn't speak Russian. But the people at the library were too busy to pay attention to me. As I walked out the door, Olga approached me and offered to help. We went to a local phone store and discovered they charged me for various services I didn't want or need. We straightened it out, walked up the block, and parted company. I thanked her very much and went home. At this point, she was one of the many students who helped me with my problems.

After our class finished, my students invited me to the café at the library to get some coffee and continue our discussion. I wasn't sure what I wanted when Olga approached me and told me I should try some Ruff Coffee, the coffee of Russia. I turned around and looked at her. Our eyes held together, and I realized our "antenna" had met. When things were finally over between us, I went to the café and had some Ruff Coffee, and I remembered her and that first day it all started.

Soon, she began to have dinner with me at a nearby restaurant. Then, she invited me to the theater, and as she leaned toward me to translate the Russian, I felt drawn to her and knew she was drawn to me. Finally, a few months before New Year's Eve, we walked around Red Square to see the fantastic decorations. There, I decided to tell her that I was a lesbian. She said nothing, and I left it for her to consider.

After I began to open up to her about my lesbian tendencies, she began to open up about her sex life. She had had a non-sexual relationship with two young men when she was younger. One left her. The second used to take her clothes off and kiss her all over but never had sexual contact with her. After a while, he went with no explanation.

Her relationship with women was far more subtle and sensual. As a young girl, she used to go under the table with her friend and spend hours gently touching each other. She had a similar relationship with her college roommate. She pushed her bed next to this woman's, and they lay there for hours, touching each other before they went to sleep. It, again, was a sensual and not a sexual experience. It went on for four years, at which point Olga felt the need to get married and so to search for a husband. When the other woman found out, she became very jealous, but this did not stop Olga from searching for her husband.

I must have sensed what she wanted because touching became my signature gesture after Olga had an orgasm: I move close to her and touch her all over her body: her straight hair, the delicate curls of her ears, the slope of her nose, and the soft sinew of her neck, threw which the pulse of life rushed: her lips which had just touched me, her slim thighs and the long suppleness of her calves; all the parts I had played so perfectly to bring her to satisfaction a few moments before. I would do this for hours until it was time for her to leave and go home to her husband.

She met her husband, Michael, when she was deeply involved with the Russian Orthodox Church. I don't remember when she became so involved, but it was a sudden change in her life, for she had been raised an atheist. Her husband, too, had once been raised as an atheist but was now a devoted member of the Russian Orthodox Church. He and Olga developed a relationship and married. He was a virgin, and so was she, and there was a wealth of information they had to learn to make love to one another; information they did not even know existed, so problems emerged right from the beginning. She delivered her son Matthew at home. She devoted her life to Matthew for nearly two years, but then, as she said, "she became quite bored with him" and wanted to move on. The tendency to become bored with someone is a pattern in her life.

Olga and I used to wonder whether Michael was gay because he wanted nothing to do with her genitals. He rarely, if ever, touched her in that way, and if he did, she found it unsatisfactory, and he was repulsed. Thus, from the beginning of her marriage, she was a woman who felt rejected by her husband because she possessed the genitals of a woman, which was offensive to him.

Neither did he pay attention to her; he was always lost on the web, playing games, or replying to someone about religion. In his spart time he practiced drums or guitar. He lived in a world of his own. She felt, in a word, unloved and uncared for, which was something she was familiar with. His only saving grace was that he supported her and her children. In keeping with the Church's tenets, it was his responsibility to take care of his family and hers to care for the children. She nagged him continuously about his duties to them.

In the 8th month of her second pregnancy, Michael had an affair. He wanted to marry this woman, as he could not have sex with her unless they were married. He would leave Olga, who was "not the kind of woman men wrote poems about" but was a nag who constantly yelled at him.

It was true; Olga, who never nagged or criticized anyone, was brutal with her husband and Matthew. She always yelled at them, and her rage would boil over into violence against them. On the other hand, her daughter was never hit and yelled at. I do not understand why, except that she was a lesbian and hated men. But that is too simple an explanation.

She responded to her husband's affair in a way that was in keeping with her need to be self-sacrificing: she took him to see the woman when and if he wanted Olga waited for him to come home from her house, and she tried, in a word, to make herself subservient to his needs: obedient, helpful, even kind. After a time, Michael went to see their priest and was told that a man had to stay married and faithful no matter what, so he gave up on his girlfriend and returned to Olga. Olga said that Michael had returned to her, which was enough, but it was not sufficient, for several times when she was on vacation, Michael sat in his girlfriend's car until late at night. He never brought her into the house because I watched everything from my apartment, but he sat with her every evening until Olga came home.

It took a few weeks for Olga to decide about having an affair with me. She did not back away from me as she would have; we grew closer. We went one day to look for hair jewelry to put into a braid, for I wore a braid behind my left ear and let it grow until I could put jewelry in it. Olga found a jewelry store, and we traveled there to see what they had. We picked out some things, and then we walked near a mirror. Olga asked me to look in the mirror, and I told her I was not too fond of mirrors because I didn't particularly appreciate how I looked when I was older. Her response was to say to me she liked how I looked. I leaned over and kissed her.

The next time we met, she was taking me home and going to do my nails. We leaned into each other, and she did my nails very slowly, very carefully, and then when she finished putting her things away, Olga looked at me and cast a "come hither" look. I shut off the lights, and we kissed each other for the first time. The next day, in the evening, we made love.

But this was not how our relationship started, for it was not gentle touching but a cruel sadism that dominated our relationship. Olga always talked about the men in Michael's life; he was an architect and interacted with his clients at home. Initially, I thought this was a reason for my jealousy, as she always felt that these men were attracted to her and preferred her company to that of Michael. Olga told me about one man, whose name I can't remember, who wanted to be alone with her. I got extremely jealous, as I did not understand that her need to be approved by the men was just another way of showing how desirable she was. What she wanted was for everyone to like and desire her. But at the time, I would get hugely jealous of the men attracted to her. I tied her up and punished her.

I had been her lover for several months when COVID-19 spread across Moscow, and we were told we would have to stay home after a specific date. It was enough that we should meet several times a week, see each other in class, and have dinner afterward. I hated when she brought her family into our relationship, talking about her husband and children. But now everything would change, and Olga started to ask me if I would come and live with her until the virus was over. I did not want to do this, but Olga convinced me that I could not stay in my apartment alone and it would be better if I came and lived with her as she had an apartment over the garage, which was furnished and empty. At least I had a fenced-in area that I could walk around in, and we would get food delivered. Well, I thought, this would only be for a few months; I could put up with her family for that long.

For both of us, it was sheer joy because we could see each other when we wanted, as there was no need to wait for an evening together. We would spend time in their beautiful, fenced-in yard, have dinner, or sit around and gaze at each other when no one was around. When the spring came, I started a garden, and Olga, who was not very interested in gardening, started making trellises for the peas. I watched her with fascination and delight as she did it. When it got warmer, we went for walks to the Moscow River, which was nearby, or swimming in the pond next door. In the heat of summer, we spent our time getting exercise for the turtle, which someone had given her son. She would watch it until it threatened to go away and then pick it up, and then it was my turn. In the evening, she would either wait for her husband to sleep or make up an excuse so we could make love. Life was wonderful.

Chapter 35: Memories of Olga's Family

Although I did not lie to Michael, Olga did so quite professionally. It was easy as Michel had a brain that interpreted things mystically and magically. He believed in the Bible and Aliens. He showed me pictures of aliens on YouTube and dared me to tell him I was wrong. These were, of course, the mummies of children left behind for sacrifice. in some Latin American countries. He believed what everyone told him: that there was a woman who had magical powers and could get rid of any illness, that if you wished hard enough, you could get what you wanted, which was being rich. Olga was endlessly trying to get him not to spend money on frivolous things that didn't work, and mostly, she succeeded. It was easy to get someone to believe you who believes in magical thinking, and so Michael thought everything that Olga told him.

Because of the closeness to her family, we stopped enjoying the sadistic part of our relationship and settled into a more normal relationship. I loved to please her, and it seemed as if that was enough for me, and in turn, she pleased me, more or less, and it was sufficient for us. The great joy came when, after satisfying her, I touched her all over her body, and she lay peaceful and still. The need to be touched was so important to her.

But occasionally, our sadomasochistic relationship continued when her husband and children were gone. Then, we would engage in a long, slow, drawn fantasy in which pleasure and pain became indiscernible. I would touch her softly to give her pleasure, and then I would find some soft, vulnerable spot and press it until it hurt. We stayed this way for hours until we were no longer in this world but in another, where we lay senseless and timeless.

When I walked in and met their daughter, Miya, I knew her for what she was: a psychopath in training. As she tried to tell Olga, she and no one else was responsible for the family's behavior. She was cruel, mean, authoritarian, and violent in her behavior towards others. She would get a stick and hit her father; she got in fights with her brother, who tried to calm the situation as, no matter what, he would get beaten for her actions. With Olga, she too exhibited sadomasochistic behavior of hitting her mother and kissing and licking her in seconds. The licking was her way of giving affection to Olga, and it did seem to me to have lesbian tendencies.

On one occasion, Michael missed his daughter, who was on vacation with his mother, and asked Olga if she also missed her. Olga answered that if Miya were there, he would stop saying that. But it was the truth; he missed Miya so much whenever she was away. His children, and Miya in particular, were the joy of his life. He loved to have them sleep with him. Olga and I used to wonder when he told her that Miya told him he was handsome or when she kissed him or showed him affection because it seemed he had a crush on his daughter, not his wife.

Michael was missing Miya so much that he would call Miya and speak to her and ask Olga to join him. I was sitting downstairs with Olga when he called, and upon being asked, Olga left me and went upstairs. Her daughter, who missed her so much, started to cry when she saw her. In response, Olga went downstairs, unable to deal with Miya's tears. As she left the room, Michael called her something in Russian that meant a heartless person. Olga came downstairs, cried to me, and complained about what he had done. In telling the truth and calling Olga heartless, he returned to her pain at being confronted with her authentic self.

But moving in with Olga and her family reignited my overall narcissistic and sadistic tendencies, and I became unbearable and critical. I criticized her and her husband for whatever they were doing that did not seem appropriate. I found fault with many of their behavior: everything from how they treated their employees to how they kept the kitchen to the general filth around the house, which

Michael lived with, and Olga tried to clean. She was, herself, particularly upset by the fact that Michael and his son did not help in cleaning up; in fact, Michael's mother lived in a wallow of filth, and he had grown up in it, and so, it did not matter if he dropped his sweater on the floor. It laid there, or if he didn't put his clothes away. It mattered a great deal to Olga because she was obsessive-compulsive about cleaning. He came from an unbearable, filthy mother and married an obsessively clean woman. I sided with Olga on this, but I was becoming involved in a situation I didn't like but could not respond to any other way than by telling them what I thought they should do, no matter how crudely or roughly. They were both passive people and accepted my judgment because I was older and wiser.

As for the boy, Matthew, he rarely becomes angry, but like his mother, he is depressed and subtly aggressive. When he didn't want to do homework or chores, he became depressed and cried. I didn't quite understand the nature of depression because it was not a part of my makeup. People, particularly in my family, except Tiel, who was bipolar, seldom got depressed. But Olga would cry at the drop of a hat: she cried because her husband called her names, whether these names were justified or not. I, annoyed, used to ask her what she was crying about, not understanding any of it. I had been raised not to cry. Matthew mimicked her depression, and often used sadness as a means of getting what he wanted from her

While Miya was exempt from all punishment, Michael beat Matthew for not doing his homework, hitting his sister when she started the fight, and not doing what he was told to do. He was beaten almost every day by Michael and Olga. I saw this once when Olga, seeing no one was around, just started wailing away at Matthew for who knows what. First, one hand and then when she missed the other, until he fell to the floor. I had caught her not being the good person she would have the world think she was. I had made the ultimate criticism

I could: she was a bad mother. It was the beginning of the end of my relationship with Olga.

At this time, and partially due to my criticism of her, she took Matthew to a psychiatrist who asked her whether she wanted her son to jump out of a window because he was so depressed. As I later realized, his head would sometimes slump forward in a classic sign of depression.

Shortly thereafter, Olga said Michael wanted to speak to me. He and Olga came down, and one sat on one side of the table from me, and the other sat at the other. Essentially, he told me he wanted more money than I was paying. I had agreed to pay him something when I was there because it was a matter of pride; I would not live at Michael's for nothing. I also would have given Olga as much money as she needed, within reason, if she had asked me. But she and Michael have demanding it from me and as I knew, this was Olga's idea. There I was, sitting between the two of them, and I felt like a stranger, like someone who stood alone against the both of them, who were a pair. This was the first sign that something had come between Olga and me.

I would move as quickly as possible but then thought better of it. What would I do without Olga, or more precisely, without my need for Olga? I stayed and gave them the money but no longer bothered to cook for the family twice daily. Instead, I stayed in my apartment, ordered groceries, and lived alone. Olga would come by when she could, and we would make love, but the niceties between us were over.

At last, Olga kept her children away from me, and I, in turn, kept to myself teaching and writing. We came together only to have sex and perhaps enjoy some time in the evening. In December, Olga spent much of her time with her family, and visiting friends in the suburbs of the city. I was not asked and did not want to go. It was a further sign that our relationship was over.

When she came back, she took Matthew to do a film in the Moscow suburbs. She told me to wait for her to have sex. I waited and waited and finally called her find out where she was. She said later that she didn't want to speak to me because she would have to speak English. I thought to myself, how strange that she would not want to speak English when everyone was impressed with someone who spoke English fluently. When she came to see me the next day, she told me a long story about a woman she saw in the street who was being threatened and so she had to stop and help her. I knew this was a crock of shit, and I told her so. Her response was well, that is what she told me, and if I didn't believe her, "I would never know for sure, would I?" I knew she was lying, but I was unsure what or why.

Our anniversary was coming up, and Olga asked if she could go and visit her friend, also named Olga, a few miles away. I said sure, but I was certain now that she had something else on her mind. Her friend, Olga, was a Russian Orthodox woman with many children, both boys and girls. My Olga said that she would speak about the problems of raising a boy to the woman who was coming over. This was ridiculous, as Olga was there to talk about the difficulties of raising a son. My response was, "Who was she to tell anyone how to raise her son when she was just learning herself?" I thought then that it was her girlfriend, the one she met at the children's film, who she would see. I knew that my worst nightmare, that of losing Olga, was going to happen.

Olga had then decided to go on vacation with the kids; she was going to visit a friend upstate, and though I wanted to go, she wanted to be alone with the children. She returned from her holiday but not at the woman's upstate home, but from Turkey; she had arrangements to go to Turkey way before. Olga had gone on vacation with her children and with her girlfriend and child. She had already abandoned me.

On a Sunday late in February, Olga took the car to the shop and didn't invite me. She said she had a lot of work to do as she was translating for another company. I knew where she was. Not consciously, but unconsciously, I knew. Sunday was her day to visit her girlfriend, and she would make up some excuses.

It seemed like my whole world, every part of it was falling apart. I had gotten fired from my critical thinking class at the library because, as it turned out, what I was teaching had offended Putin's people, who were more rigorously imposing anyone who dared to challenge them. I was, after all, preaching communism to my students in an era in which the Oligarchs, as they were called, took the wealth of the state for themselves, and the average person was left behind with neither the ideology nor the practice of communism. I was preaching a return to communism as a better way of life, and people were listening to me. It took them a while to figure this out, but when they did, I was doomed.

They had called me twice to warn me; this was the third time. Even the people in charge of the library wrote to tell me that I had taught "wonderful classes" and earned the "respect of my students." It was not my teaching that offended them, but the idea of what I was teaching: the return to communism. I told my students that I would start teaching critical thinking on the web, only to be receive a letter that said if you were not involved with a Russian institution, you could not teach online. I had no choice but to close my online classes. Olga helped me with the process on a Saturday, and I woke up with a stroke on Sunday. On Monday we went to the hospital, unsure what was wrong with me. I knew I could not speak.

I went to the hospital and was admitted. I was treated for a stroke to my brain, which resulted in aphasia, and spent nearly three weeks in the hospital. While I was there, Olga tried her best to help me, sitting with the therapist, who spoke no English, and translating things for me, but I couldn't understand the difference between a dog and a cat. I couldn't understand anything. I got out of the hospital three days before when Olga arranged for me to go to America, for I had to go home to get help for my aphasia. We made love every evening even when I felt I could not; she seemed to want it, and I wanted to please her. I tried to speak to her so badly and tell her so many things. I wanted to say goodbye but could not. We hugged and kissed at the airport, and

Olga put me and the physician she had hired on the plane, and I left for my country. This would be the last time I would hold Olga.

Chapter 36: Memories of Going Home Again

I can't tell you what the hell it was to go home. I had a bladder infection and so had to go to the hospital. When I went there, they put me in and treated me like I had not had a stroke in Russia. Two days in the hospital cost me thousands of dollars because I had no coverage for Medicare part A. Meanwhile, I stayed in the hospital in Russia for three months, and it was free as Russia has free health care. When I got home, I was placed in a room next to the dining room and near the living room. I had to listen to my son-in-law's big mouth and the sounds of the children and grandchildren playing video games. In the evening, they watched baseball and cheered. I was recovering from a stroke and wanted only to rest. On Mother's Day, Tiel went out with her aunt instead of spending time with me and had Brooke come over to watch me. Brooke expected us to have dinner, but nope. We went searching for food but found none. In the morning, Tiel was supposed to go out and do something and then come home to go shopping. She was gone for three hours, and I, on a diabetic diet, decided to eat some fruit. As I was eating it, I felt another stroke coming on. This one affected my eyes and left me partially blind. The only thing I wanted was to go back to Olga and Russia.

I hired the woman who came to help me with the Aphasia to work with me full-time. She was a good teacher, and I was a dedicated student. In six months, I had conquered my aphasia and could speak nearly fluently. With all the COVID around, I did my best to get a plane to Russia, got my vaccinations, and made a reservation. I would get my apartment not far from Olga's and have her in my arms again.

All the while I was in America, I called her every evening, and we talked about the dreams she had at night, about her children, about her life. And I, in turn, told her about mine. I told her that I was half blind from another stroke. I have had so many strokes, and I suggested that perhaps I was too ill to have as a girlfriend. I gave her every opportunity to leave. But she clung to me, and every time I talked to her, I told her I loved her, and she told me that she loved me. She told me once, "I love you more than I have ever loved anyone," and I believed her.

Chapter 37: Memories of Returning to Olga

My friend Sergei picked me up at the airport near his house, and I spent the next three days sleeping. Olga called, as I needed her to have me registered. I expected her to come and hug her and kiss each other\, especially after all the hell I had been through in America. Instead, she told me to take a taxi. When I got there, she was surrounded by people who were waiting for an appointment. It turned out she had gone to the wrong place. But I noticed that she did not hug or kiss me. We got into the car, and again, she was unresponsive to me. When we got to place for registration we walked up, I sat on a bench while she filled out the forms, and I registered. She still was not speaking to me. As soon as we got out, I said to her, "This is it. It's over." And she said "yes." She called a cab and put me into it, and I went home to Sergei's. I did not cry.

I got another apartment in a shitty area of Moscow and stayed there for the next five months. Aside from a journey to Kyrgyzstan to get another passport, and to go shopping for food, I stayed in my apartment and tried to understand what had happened between Olga and me. There were not words for the sadness I felt; for the fact that I did not have Olga around me, to laugh and joke with, to care for me and let me care for her, to listen and be listened to, I was truly alone.

I watched every video I could and read every book I could find. I also began my autobiography about my wonderful and interesting life. It seemed like a good thing to do in my spare time. It was in the course of writing that I realized that I was not a wonderful person leading an interesting and exciting life, but that I was also a psychopath. The awareness was shocking to me. I had inflicted an incredible amount of cruelty on my children, on other people's children, on pets, on men and women who I considered to be inferior to me and yes, on Olga.

To be sure, Olga, with her personality, never told me why she ended our relationship until very recently. Almost a year after we were finished, one year of not talking to her, when all I wanted was to speak to her, she finally told me, "I guess it is easier to imagine a lover and put all the responsibility on that. But we clearly destroyed one another whether you like it or not." I understood what she meant and apologized to her for my cruelty, my sadism. I apologized to her for being a psychopath.

I employed critical thinking to deal with people all my life. People all had something wrong with them, and it was my task to figure out what it was and tell them about it. With Olga, it began when we first went on vacation together to Turkey, and I told her there was a world of difference between our sadomasochism and the hurting of Michael and Matthew, which was wrong. It was the first time, but not the last time I hurt her with my words. We were on the way to dinner, and she took out her phone and walked around the dinner area as if she were talking to someone. She was distraught because I had told her something that reflected poorly on her, and she could not handle it.

When I moved in with her and her family, it extended to a definition of telling them what was wrong with them. In the case of Olga and Michael, they submitted because I was older and wiser. It grew stronger until I told Olga what was wrong with her as a mother. I did not have to do any of this; if I did, I could learn to say things with greater regard for the person I was talking with. However, I loved telling the truth, even when it harmed people, or instead because it harmed people.

It was why I was so attracted to teaching Critical Thinking. I would find out what was wrong with someone, not to understand or improve them, but to let the person know I was superior. I had to make others look small by making myself look large, just as I had with my children, just as I had with other people's children, just as I had with animals, just as I had with men and women whom I felt were inferior to me, just as I had with my students. The only reason I did not kill someone was because the leviathans was with me, but I certainly would have, and I certainly should have. I was the only thing that mattered in the world.

In his article, The Hidden Suffering of the Psychopath by Willem H.J. Martens, M.D., Ph.D., director of the W. Kahn n Institute of Theoretical Psychiatry and Neuroscience and advisor of the Forensic Psychiatry Hospital in Assen, in The Netherlands, goes through the list of diagnostic features of a Psychopath such as "superficial charm, high intelligence, poor judgment and failure to learn from experience, pathological egocentricity and incapacity for love, lack of remorse or shame, impulsivity, grandiose sense of self-worth, pathological lying, manipulative behavior, poor self-control, promiscuous sexual behavior, juvenile delinquency, and criminal versatility among others" (Cleckley, 1982; Hare et al., 1990). I do not fulfill all of the diagnostic criteria, but I did fulfill the great majority of them. I have "the image of a cold, heartless, inhuman being" as I have stated above and expounded through the book.

Martens does have some sympathy even for these people because no matter how cold they are, they show a modicum of "emotional capacities and empathy." "Like healthy people, many psychopaths love their parents, spouse, children, and pets in their own way but have difficulty loving and trusting the rest of the world." It was not the case with me: I did not love my parents, my spouse, my pets, but I did, to a greater or lesser extent, love my children and Olga. I did suffer because of my separation from them. I am lost without them in my life.

I ride my pony across the great steps of Mongolia, following Jebe to the next conquest. I will follow the hoard as they rape, pillage, burn and destroy their enemies. Except for the women we want, the slaves we choose to serve us, and the intellectuals we spare for the sake of the Khan, we will kill them all. It is the war of all against all, and I am the conqueror who wins a pyrrhic victory. In the end, I have nothing to show for my life. I have fulfilled my destiny, and I am, as I have always been, alone.

---

[1]

Don't miss out!

Visit the website below and you can sign up to receive emails whenever Mary Metzger publishes a new book. There's no charge and no obligation.

https://books2read.com/r/B-A-HEQCB-HJLTC

BOOKS 2 READ

Connecting independent readers to independent writers.

About the Author

At 76, Mary Metzger sat down to write her autobiography. To be sure, she had lived a remarkable life:

she grew up in the hills of Pennsylvania with her grandmother and grandfather and spoke no English yet went on to become a college professor. At the age of fourteen she was a second chef. In her forties, she began a wholesale health food business that she ran for fifteen years. She had been married twice, once to a union carpenter and the second time to a hospital administrator, and had three daughters, five grandchildren, and two great grandchildren.

She traveled to over 35 countries in Europe, South America, and Africa. At the age of sixty-two, she went to live in Moscow and stayed there for sixteen years. There she met the great love of her life. The ending of this last relationship caused her to examine her existence with greater clarity. She realized that she was not only the wonderful and exciting person she claimed to be, but was in her hidden self, a psychopath. She found that she took great pleasure in inflicting cruelty on others: on her children, her husbands, her lovers, her students, in fact, on everyone in order to feel superior to them. She cared nothing about the feelings of others, but only of herself.

It was Mary herself who contributed to the development of her disease. She was responsible for the way she was. Despite her outward arrogance, inside, she felt inferior to others. She came to realize that her behavior stigmatized her and that there was nothing she could do about it.

www.ingramcontent.com/pod-product-compliance
Lightning Source LLC
Chambersburg PA
CBHW060916140726
47996CB00001B/269